English Situational Conversations
on Architectural Campus & Life Abroad

建筑校园与国外生活
英语情景会话

盛根有 著

中国建筑工业出版社

图书在版编目（CIP）数据

建筑校园与国外生活英语情景会话/盛根有著. —北京：
中国建筑工业出版社，2011.8
ISBN 978 - 7 - 112 - 13300 - 0

Ⅰ.①建…　Ⅱ.①盛…　Ⅲ.①建筑工程 – 英语 – 口语
Ⅳ.①H319.9

中国版本图书馆 CIP 数据核字（2011）第 148025 号

　　《建筑校园与国外生活英语情景会话》属于实用建筑英语情景会话系列丛书之一，该书是迄今为止在建筑业中尚未有的建筑实用英语会话专著。全书分两部，共 20 个情景对话单元。第一部　建筑校园英语情景会话，共 9 个情景对话单元，涉及建筑院校的专业以及课程设置、英语以及计算机等公共课的学习、求职与面试等必不可少同时又无法回避会话内容。第二部　建筑施工人员国外生活英语情景会话，共 11 个情景对话单元，涉及建筑施工人员国外生活的衣、食、住、行等方面会话内容。全书具有四大特点：英汉对照、音标注音、短文翻译、专业词语替换与参考。

　　本书是针对建筑院校的学生、也是为涉外建筑企业各类人员学习的专用教材；同样适用于建筑出国劳务、工程承包的技术人员、管理干部和技术工人培训的选定教材以及建筑业的广大职工学习建筑英语、渴望提高建筑英语口语会话水平，必选、必备、必读、必用之书。

*　　*　　*

责任编辑：程素荣　　责任设计：赵明霞　　责任校对：陈晶晶　刘　钰

English Situational Conversations
on Architectural Campus & Life Abroad

建筑校园与国外生活英语情景会话
盛根有　著

*
中国建筑工业出版社出版、发行（北京西郊百万庄）
各地新华书店、建筑书店经销
北京嘉泰利德公司制版
北京市密东印刷有限公司印刷
*
开本：880×1230 毫米　1/32　印张：8¼　字数：268 千字
2011 年 9 月第一版　　2011 年 9 月第一次印刷
定价：**25.00** 元
ISBN 978 - 7 - 112 - 13300 - 0
（20751）

序

　　初阅了**实用建筑英语情景会话**系列丛书即《建筑校园与国外生活英语情景会话》、《建筑技术与管理英语情景会话》和《建筑施工现场英语情景会话》有诸多感受和启发，颇为深刻的有下列几点并将其权作为序：

　　一、及时　该丛书正是在举国上下纪念改革开放三十周年，迎接建国六十周年之际出版的。出版得及时就在于，这是为中国建筑大军走向国际市场并取得辉煌成就；也是为中国建筑面临更大国际机遇与挑战；更是为保持中国建筑发展的强劲势头而出版的。这套丛书的出版，无疑将使人人通专业的广大建设者，个个也会讲英语，使他们如虎添翼，这必将在中国建设者和外国同行直接交谈工作中起着积极而又决定性的作用。无论哪位从事建筑的决策者或高管都清楚提高了建筑英语会话水平，将有助于提高中国建筑参与国际竞争的软实力从而实现发展的硬道理。

　　二、必要　本丛书的问世填补了中国建筑科技英语口语教材的空白。同时为在校学习建筑类专业的大中专学生提供了一套学以致用的好教材，尤其解决了长期以来建筑业广大工程技术人员、管理干部和各类技术工人想学习建筑英语、更想提高其会话水平却苦于无书之难。我深信只要通过对这套系列丛书认真地学习和在实践中的应用，会逐步显现出该丛书为中国建筑在国际竞争中所发挥的现实作用以及所起到的长远历史效应。

　　三、实用　这套系列丛书体现了以实用为主，以应用为目的指导原则。全书100多个情景会话单元涉及：开工前的准备，施工期间具体施工细节以及完工后的索赔和签发完工证书等内容。这些都是作者多年从事建筑翻译工作与业主、工程监理、建筑专家以及配合施工的人员打交道的真实工作写照。只有像盛先生这样有着三十多年从教经验和担任建筑翻译的经历，具有扎实英语功底又有多部个人建筑英语专著的复合型学者，才能创作出这部实用性的好作品。如果您有幸使用了该书，也有可能在国外施工过或正在国外施工，您一定会感到这套丛书用语简单便于上口，语言地道符合英美英语口语表达习惯和特点，能真正解决施工中出现的实际而又具体的问题。而且您也会清楚认识到该丛书从头到尾贯穿着"实用"两个字，从涉外建筑企业施工特点出发，着眼于施工实际，又服务于施工。

四、新颖　该丛书是作者集教学实践和翻译经验，又科学地融心理学、教育学于一体，用新理念、新思维、新方法而进行的大胆尝试。全书虽有百万余字，但这只是个固定的数字，要满足复杂多变的涉外建筑不同场合用语是远远不够的。可是既要满足需要、又要收效好才是作者追求的目标和精心设计的用心。因此，作者在这套丛书中推出情景会话教学法。百余个"学说英语情景对话"单元就是对施工环节的细化，把读者引入具体语境之中，使其在语境中能有一种身临其境的感觉，自然而然地把所学的语言知识转化为实际言语，恰如其分，自然而不做作地表达出来，会收到事半功倍的效果。在口语练习中还设计出替换练习法，把在建筑技术、管理、施工诸多方面使用频率高，却在许多英语书中又难以兼容的词语采用替换句中黑体字的方法进行练习。使用这一练习法的目的就是要把呆死的语言变成活的语言，把有限的句子变成无限的句子，起到举一反三之效果。许多人都知道"中国不愁买不到书，中国急需有创新书"，也许这部系列丛书就是您所需要的具有创意的实用书籍之一吧。

李竹成

中国建设教育协会　理事长

2009年9月于北京

前　　言

　　《建筑校园与国外生活英语情景会话》属于实用建筑英语情景会话系列丛书之一，该书是在中国改革开放中孕育，着力解决施工实际困难、促进生产力快速发展的知识创新中诞生，又在与时俱进中逐步完善，科学发展中不断升华。《建筑校园与国外生活英语情景会话》着眼于提高中国建筑参与国际竞争的软实力，为拓宽中国建筑在世界建筑市场的占有率，并保持强劲发展势头，从而实现中国建筑良性发展的硬实力；为解决建筑院校的学员想学习、要提高建筑英语会话水平却苦于无书之难；也为弥补建筑业广大职工专业英语会话水平之差；更是着力改变目前涉外广大施工人员英语会话水平特别薄弱的缺憾。这一缺憾已成为涉外施工头号难题——语言障碍。人人像聋子、个个如哑巴的涉外施工人员有口却不会说，有耳却听不懂的被动，尴尬而又特别无奈的实际困难而精心撰写的。

　　由于我国已经过三十年的改革开放，企业管理，用人机制等方面在现代企业中都已步入科学化、规范化，所以作为现代建筑人不仅要有过硬技术以保质保量保进度搞好施工，还要有能为自身服务和发展的英语水平。这是时代对现代建筑人的起码要求，也是为落实国际施工合同规定的工作用语——英语所采取的举措。目的就是要让广大建筑施工人员在未来的施工中与监理和相关人员能进行一般性的工作语言交流，改写中国建筑人与外国专家在施工中无法用语言直接交谈和沟通的历史。再说要想学好《建筑技术与管理英语情景会话》或《建筑施工现场英语情景会话》，首先得学习而且得学好《建筑校园与国外生活英语情景会话》，因为它包括有学好口语会话必须掌握的语音知识、构词法、基本专业词语和基本口语交际用语等内容，所以它是学习和掌握《建筑技术与管理英语情景会话》或《建筑施工现场英语情景会话》的基础。

《建筑校园与国外生活英语情景会话》分两部：第一部　建筑校园英语情景会话，涉及到建筑院校的专业与课程设置、英语以及计算机等公共课的学习、求职与面试等必不可少而又无法回避内容。第二部　建筑施工人员国外生活英语情景会话，涉及到建筑施工人员国外生活的衣、食、住、行等方方面面的英语会话内容。本书无论从选题到具体内容，都切合学校实际，突出国外生活应用，作到有的放矢不放空炮。这也正是作者苦心创作该书的初衷。假如您有国外工作的经历或有幸亲临施工现场目睹了建设者是怎样施工的，您一定会感到《建筑校园与国外生活英语情景会话》是怎样满足您国外实际生活的需要，为您当好向导；又怎样为您铺垫学好该丛书。这套丛书是作者真实的工作写照，也是作者融实用性与科学性，集知识性与创造性于一体形成的独树一帜创作新思维、新理念，更是作者几十年潜心研究向社会递交的答卷；是把教育理论运用于教学实践的尝试，是把公共英语融入专业英语的创新，是把经验变成实践的产物。本书在句子方面回避了长句而用短句做到了口语化，简单又直接；在用词语方面避开了书面语选用了口语词语所以便于上口、讲起来地道、符合英美英语口语表达习惯和特点。读者可立刻将书中的内容用到工作中，也可就某一具体问题现学现用，会收到事半功倍、立竿见影的效果。可以说"一书在手万事不求，施工交谈无须发愁"。

该书具有下列四大特点：

1. 英汉对照：全书情景对话单元——学说英语是作者在这套丛书中推出的情景会话教学法。全书情景对话均采用英汉对照的模式给读者展示出英汉两种语言的不同表达方式。通过对照和比较会一目了然地看到这两种语言并非 1+1 就完全等于 2，而是各自有着各自表达特点、方式和习惯。使读者懂得在哪种语言情景中说哪些话，用哪些词语更得体、更恰当、更准确，并采用哪种语体、语气、语态和外国人进行交谈更合适、更习惯，收到的效果会更理想。

2. 音标注音：全书口语练习中的专业词语均注有国际音标，每个词语都是根据《新英汉词典》和《现代高级英汉双解辞典》注音，以满足不同程度读者能按照国际音标规范发音的需要，使其不仅能规范发音而且保障发音准确，为今后轻松上口，确保口语水平既循序渐进又能扎扎实实稳步提高铺平了道路。

3. 短文翻译：该书口语练习中均设有短文翻译（英汉互译）。设立这些短文翻译练习的目的不仅在于训练学生对翻译技巧的运用，以培养其翻译能力，更重要的是通过翻译获取相关的专业词汇和专业知识，拓宽视野，为未来专业的发展奠定了基础。

4. 专业词语替换与参考：全书在口语练习中设计出替换练习法。这些替换与参考词语是根据每个情景对话单元实际需要而精挑细选，特意补充的，并兼有两种作用。其一是替换口语练习中黑体词语，目的是打破传统的教学模式，把一种呆死的语言变成活的语言，起到举一反三的作用；其二是为满足读者实际工作的需要，而提供的参考和备查词语，以解决施工中突如其来的实际问题而急需的词语。除此之外，在《建筑校园与国外生活英语情景会话》一书中还增加了**日常交际习语**内容，增加这一内容是为丰富和弥补不同基础学员的英语口语学习的需要。

实用建筑英语情景会话系列丛书是为学子实现知识改变命运，技能成就未来的好书，更是为学子终生奠基，为读者起航插翅的良师益友。

书后附录有国际音标；英美英语常用词语对照；中国人与西方人士交往应注意的事项；口语练习答案——汉语参考译文等以配合本书学习和使用时参考。

本书所有的插图均由盛莉绘制。

承蒙中国华山国际工程公司驻美国、利比亚、塞拉利昂、巴新等十国项目经理曹喜文，陕西建设技术学院常务副院长程根虎，陕西建筑职工大学副校长杨玉军，陕西建设技术学院教务主任李建军，英籍建筑教授 David S. Mcculloch 等专家型领导给予的关心和支持，在此特表示感谢！

本书不仅是土地培育的禾苗，也是工作实践的再现。1993 年动笔，披阅十五载，九易其稿，但可能仍有不尽如人意之处，疏漏和不妥在所难免，诚望广大读者、同行赐教。

盛根有

2010 年 8 月于西安

CONTENTS

【注】S. W. E. = Substitute Words & Expressions

目 录

Part One
English Conversations with Students
in Architectural Campus
(Situational Dialogic Unit 1 – 9)

第一部
建筑校园英语情景会话
（第一至第九情景对话单元）

Situational Dialogic Unit 1

第一情景对话单元

Learn to Speak English

Talking about an English Class

A. Greeting and Introduction

Herman：(It's time for class.) Now class begins.

Xiao He：Stand up!

Herman：How are you, everybody?

Students：How are you, sir?

Xiao He：Sit down!

Herman：Is there anyone absent, I'd love to know?

Xiao He：No. Everyone is present, sir.

Herman：Well, did you have a good summer holiday?

Students：Yes, of course, sir.

Herman：I'm happy to hear this. I'd like to give you an introduction myself first, OK?

Students：That would be very nice, sir.

Herman：My name is Herman and I come from far away, the United States of America (USA), that's to say America. English is my native language so I can speak fluent and idiomatic English.

Students：It's obvious and unquestionable.

Herman：Yes, I teach you oral English because I've such ability to teach this subject well.

Students：That's very kind of you. You look not only young and handsome but also humorous, so we all like you very much.

Herman：I'm indebted to you for praise. And don't look down upon mc young, I was graduated from American Harvard University in the nineties of the last century and obtain literature doctoral degree.

Students：Nobody look down on you. How great you are!

Herman：Though I've tought English more than ten years, accumulated a few teaching experience and teaching effect is fine, I must do my job well with all my heart, never be ludicrous conceit of the king of Ye-lang——parochial arrogance and don't strive for further progress.

学说英语

谈论一堂英语课

A. 打招呼与介绍

赫尔曼：（上课时间到了。）现在开始上课。

晓　柯：起立！

赫尔曼：你们大家都好吗？

学　生：您好，先生？

晓　柯：坐下！

赫尔曼：我想知道有缺课的吗？

晓　柯：没有，都到了，先生。

赫尔曼：那么，暑假过得都很愉快吧？

学　生：当然是，先生。

赫尔曼：我也很高兴听到这些。我来先给你们做个自我介绍好吗？

学　生：那可太好啦，先生。

赫尔曼：我叫赫尔曼，来自遥远的美利坚合众国，也就是美国。英语是我的母语，所以我能讲一口流利而又地道的英语。

学　生：这是显而易见的也是无可置疑的。

赫尔曼：是的，我给你们上英语口语课，因为我具备了上好这门课的能力。

学　生：那可太好啦。看上去你既年轻又英俊而且还很幽默，我们都挺喜欢你的。

赫尔曼：承蒙夸奖。可不要看我很年轻，我可是 20 世纪 90 年代毕业于美国哈佛大学，并获得了文学博士学位。

学　生：没人小看你。你可真棒呀！

赫尔曼：尽管我已从事了十多年英语教学工作，积累了一些教学经验，教学效果也很不错，但我还得尽心搞好本职工作，决不能夜郎自大，不求进取。

Students: Don't say any words of courtesy. We all know this and believe your ability to teach us well. Thank you for your introduction.

Herman: It's nothing. From now on, I'm your teacher of English and we'll study and live together. Please tell me soon if you need some help—both public affairs and private interests, especially English studying, Please point out timely.

Students: Why do you take good care of us, sir?

Herman: That's my duty bound because I'm your teacher.

Students: Thank you. Welcome to our class! We must cooperate well with you, improve teaching & learning work.

Herman: I'm satisfied with your answer. Only by teaching and learning two actives can be fully mobilized and played well, teaching & learning work must be improved, and teaching value can be reflected and learning significance too, teaching level must be embodied and learning result either. Do you think what I said is reasonable?

Students: Certainly. We think so.

B. Signalling Stages in the Lesson

Herman: Well. Let's make a long story short and return our subject. In this period class, we're going to do aural-comprehension training first, that's to say, practise with audio-visual aids, and then spend some time for situational dialogue, that topical title is George Washington. Do you all know my meaning?

Students: Yes. To develop our ability to listening and speaking.

Herman: Quite well. Let me tell you main idea about the listening material the first, shall I?

Students: OK. That's fine. Please say so, sir.

Herman: The story is about the first President of America——George Washington how to study in his childhood. I hope my prompting can give you much help in your hearing and seeing so much.

Students: Thank you for the prompt. We must listen and watch conscientiously.

学　生：客套话就甭再说啦，我们都知道了、也相信你有能力教好我们。感谢您的自我介绍。

赫尔曼：没什么。从现在起，我就是你们的英语老师了，我们在一起学习和生活。如有什么要我帮的，不管公事还是私事，我都会尽力而乐意去做，特别是在英语学习方面，请给我及时提出来。

学　生：您为什么要这样呵护着我们，先生？

赫尔曼：因为我是你们的老师，所以这是我义不容辞的义务。

学　生：谢谢您。欢迎给我们班上课，我们一定配合好你，搞好教学工作。

赫尔曼：你们的回答，我很满意。只有充分调动和发挥好教和学两个积极性，才能搞好教学工作，才能体现出教的价值，学的意义，更能体现出教的水平；学的效果。你们认为我说得有道理吗？

学　生：是的，有道理。

B. 表明授课环节

赫尔曼：好啦。咱们还是长话短说，言归正传吧。这节课我们先进行听视训练，也就是用听视教具进行练习，然后再花点儿时间进行情景会话。听视训练的主题是乔治·华盛顿。你们都明白用意吗？

学　生：是的，为了提高我们的听说能力。

赫尔曼：很好。我来先讲讲这个听力材料的大意好吗？

学　生：好啊，那太好啦！请讲吧，先生。

赫尔曼：这是一个关于美国首任总统乔治·华盛顿童年是怎样学习的故事。希望我的提示能对你们的听视有所帮助。

学　生：多谢您的提示。我们一定认真地进行听视。

Herman: That's all right. Now I'd like to say some requirements about aural-comprehension training.

Students: What are the requirements, please tell us, sir.

Herman: Let me tell you soon. Undoubtly, you did aural-comprehension training before, isn't it same requirement for every time of aural-comprehension training?

Students: Yes, just so. What requirement is it this time?

Herman: Take it easy! I'm about to tell you. You'll listen three times in all. You have to be absorbed in listening first, do you understand?

Students: Yes, we do. What about second time?

Herman: The requirement of the second time is on the first time. You'll take some notes while listening and in order to retell after the third time.

Students: Oh, Retelling must be done. Does the requirement demand so high?

Herman: Is it so? The requirement may be a bit high at beginning but it'll give so much advantages for your future conversation. Because any conversations must be understood what he or she said first and then you can answer them correctly. Please understand my kindness, OK?

Students: Don't worry! How couldn't we understand you? And we also know the dialectical relation from quantitative change to qualitative change.

Herman: Understanding is OK. So only through retelling I can distinguish how much you understand about it.

Students: Sound reasonable.

Herman: And then you'll retell after the third listening time. How do you think of the arrangement?

Students: Well, nice and good.

Herman: This is an aural-comprehension training step. As to hearing skills I can timely tell you when I give you my lecture. Enough of this digression; let's return to our story. Are you ready?

Students: Yeah. We're ready, sir.

Herman: Let's begin to listen now.

赫尔曼：不客气。我现在还想讲讲听力训练的相关要求。

学　生：什么要求，先生，请告诉我们吧。

赫尔曼：这就告诉你们。毫无疑问，你们以前都做过听力训练，每次的训练要求可能有所不同对吧？

学　生：是啊！是这样！那这次的要求是什么？

赫尔曼：甭着急，这就告诉你。你们总共要听三遍。第一遍要全神贯注地听，明白了吗？

学　生：是的，明白了。那第二遍呢？

赫尔曼：第二遍要求就是在第一遍的基础上，一边听一边做笔记，记下关键的词语为听完第三遍后复述做准备。

学　生：啊！还要复述，这要求可太高了吧？

赫尔曼：是吗？这一要求可能在起初有点苛刻，但这种要求对你们日后的会话是大有益处的，因为会话首先是要能听懂别人说啥，其次才是准确的回答。请理解我的一片苦心，行吗？

学　生：放心好啦！我们怎不能理解您的一片好意呢？而且我们懂得量变到质变的辩证关系。

赫尔曼：能理解就好。所以只有通过复述才能鉴别出你们究竟听懂了多少。

学　生：言之有理。

赫尔曼：那听完第三遍就复述。你们认为这一安排怎样？

学　生：啊，挺好的。

赫尔曼：这只是个听力训练的步骤，至于听力技巧，我会在以后讲课的过程中及时的告诉你们的。闲话少说，书归正传。准备好了吗？

学　生：是的，先生，准备好啦。

赫尔曼：咱们现在开始听吧。

Formulaic Communication 日常交际习语

Requests and Responses 请求与应答

1. May I ask you a question? 我可以请教你个问题吗？
   ——Certainly. 当然可以。

2. Can you do me a favour/ a favour for me? 您能帮我个忙吗？
   ——I will if I can. 如果我能的话，我一定。

3. May I borrow some books? 我可以借用几本书吗？
   ——Sure. Just help yourself. 可以，自己拿吧。

4. I wonder if you can lend me your dictionary? 我不知您能否把字典借给我用一下？
   ——I'd very much like to, but I'm afraid I can't right now. I'm looking up some words in it now. 我很愿意，但恐怕此刻不行，我正在用着呢。

5. Would you kindly/please wait for me a minute? 劳驾等我一会儿行吗？
   ——All right. 行。

6. Could you speak a little louder? 您能稍微大点声说吗？
   ——Yes, of course. 当然可以。Your request will be attended to. 我会考虑你的要求的。

7. Do you mind if I switch on/off the light? 我把灯打开/关掉你不介意吧？
   ——Not at all. Go ahead. 好，请把。
   ——I'd rather you don't. 我倒希望你不要打开/关掉。

Explanatory Notes注释：

1. teacher 这个称呼只限于对中国教师用，对外籍教师很不合适。对外籍教师应称先生/Sir、小姐/Miss、夫人/Mrs. 为佳。

2. 英语教师与英籍教师应该怎样区分又怎么称呼才对。英语教师是 a teacher of English，虽然这一叫法不为人知或许不符合中国人的思维习惯，但这却是标准的英语说法，应加以肯定。尽管 an'English teacher 也可称之为英语教师，但 English 一词一定要重读；an English'teacher 称之为英籍老师，是因为 English 轻读，而 teacher 重读，只有这样读其意才为英籍老师。

3. 对于如王老师的称呼，外国人习惯却要从性别上加以区别。如：Mr. Wang（男性）—Sir（男性）、Ms Wang（女性）—Madam（女性）、Miss Wang（未婚女性）、Mrs. Wang（已婚女性，其丈夫姓"王"）—Mistress（夫人）。按中国人习惯常称王老师为 Teacher Wang，这不符合英语表达习惯，Wang Teacher 无疑是中国式的英语。

4. 学生一词的英语译文是 pupil、student 或 class。pupil 和 student 是 teacher 的对应词。pupil 常为小学生，student 则为中或大学生。可有时在课堂上有些教师也可称全体学生为 class，以表示亲切。为了把大学生表达得更确切起见，还可以说 freshman 大学一年级学生或新生（美国英语是中学一年级学生），sophomore 大学或中学二年级学生，junior（美国中学或四年制大学中的）三年级学生，senior（美国）大学四年级学生，undergraduate 本科生，postgraduate 研究生。

Spoken Practice 口语练习

1. Pair Work：

Imagine that you're all the freshmen who learn architectural major. Maybe some of you didn't know how important English is, so they didn't study hard and well before coming to Architectural College/University. As college/University students must not only study major course well but also English. Try to work out and say your studying plan each other.

2. Answer the Following Questions in accordance with Practical Case：

1）Did you have a good summer vercation?

2）Who's your new teacher of English? Is he/she a Chinese or a foreigner?

3）What's your first unit content of this book? Try to say something about it.

4）Have your new teacher of English told you any good methods for learning English? Please give us one or two examples at least.

5）Why are you studying the Spoken Textbook of Architectural English and how can you learn it well? Try to say your view.

3. Read & Interpret the Following Passage：

How Karl Marx Studied Forenge Languages

"A foreign language is a weapon in the struggle of life." was Karl Marx's well-known saying. He regarded foreign languages as so important because he knew people go in for communication with it. With foreign languages, people can both learn and intoduce other advance science & technology and thought and his own view and thought. He both said and did so.

Marx could read all the leading European languages and could write in three——German, French and English. Marx was already fifty years old when he began studying Russian and in six months he was able to read the works of famous writers like Gogol and Pushking.

4. Learn the Following Usefull Abbreviated Words by Heart：

phr. （phrase）短语

ch/chap. （chapter）章

par.（paragraph）节；段

p.（page）页

ref.（reference）参考；依据

f. e（for example）例如

cp.（compare）比较

sb.（somebody）某人

sth.（something）某事

sp.（someplace）某处

id.（idem）同上

P. C.（per cent）百分之

5. Give the International Phonetic Symbols（国际音标）of the Following Useful Words：

单　　词	强读音标		弱读音标	
is／am／are	[iz／æm／a：]		[z／əm／ə]	
were／was	[	]	[	]
have／has／had	[	]	[	]
do／does／did	[	]	[	]
shall／should	[	]	[	]
will／would	[	]	[	]
can／could	[	]	[	]
but／as／and／or／than	[	]	[	]
by／at／for／of／from／to	[	]	[	]
such／some／any	[	]	[	]
you／／he／she／we	[	]	[	]
me／him／her／us／them	[	]	[	]
who／that	[	]	[	]
the／a／an	[	]	[	]
myself／yourself／themselves	[	]	[	]

6. Substitute the Following Words & Expressions：

1）Use the following **Some Classroom Expressions（一些课堂用语）** to replace the black words in the following sentence：

Herman：**Is there anyone absent**，I'd love to know？

赫尔曼：我想知道**有缺课的吗**？

Xiao He：No. **Everyone is present**，sir.

晓　珂：没有，**都到了**，先生。

Some Classroom Expressions 一些课堂用语

［sʌm'klɑːsru(ː)m iks'preʃənz］

Let's have a break. ［lets hæv ə briːk］ 咱们休息一会儿。

That's all for today. ［ðæts ɔːl fə tə'dei］ 今天就讲到这里。

The class is over /dismissed. ［ðə klɑːs iz 'ouvə dis'misid］ 下课。

Please pay attention/ raise your hands. ［pliːz pei ə'tenʃən reis jɔː hændz］请注意/举手

Take your time. There's no hurry. ［teik jɔːtaim ðɔəz nou'hʌri］ 慢一点，别着急。

Answer the question. ［'ʌnsə ðə 'kwesʃən］ 回答问题。

Read in chorus/after me! ［riːd in'kɔːrəs ɑː'ftə miː］ 齐声读/跟我读！

Open/close your books! ［'oupən klouz jɔː buks］ 打开/合上书！

No talking/helping! ［nou 'tɔːkiŋ'helpiŋ］ 不要说话/提示！

Prepare/Rievew your lessons! ［pri'pɛə ri'vjuː jɔː'lesnz］ 预习/复习功课！

Hand in your papers/exercise books! ［hænd in jɔː'peipəz'eksəsaiz buks］ 交作业/练习本！

have reading aloud/ a spelling check/a dictation/a translation exercise.

［hæv 'riːdiŋ ə'laud ə'speliŋ tʃek ə dik'teiʃən ə træns'leiʃən'eksəsaiz］

进行朗读/拼写检查/听写/翻译练习

2）Use the following **Teaching Expressions**（教学用语）to replace the black words in the following sentence：

Herman：And then you'll **retell** after **the third listening time.** How do you think of the arrangement？

赫尔曼：那**听完第三遍就复述**。你们认为这一安排怎样？

Teaching Expressions ［'tiːtʃiŋ iks'preʃənz］ 教学用语

at the top/bottom of the page 8 在第 8 页上面/下面。

［ət ðə tɔp 'bɔtəm əv ðə peidʒ eit］

14

near the top/bottom of the page 9 在第 9 页偏上/下。

［niə ðə tɔp ˈbɔtəm əv ðə peidʒ nain］

in the middle of the page 20 ［in ðəˈmidl əv ðə peidʒˈtwenti］

在第 20 页中间。

the third line from the bottom 倒数第三行。

［ðə θə:d lain frɔm ðəˈbɔtəm］

the next to the last line/the last line but one 倒数第二行。

［ðə nekst tu ðə la:st lain ðə la:st lain bʌt wʌn］

the third /fourth/fifth... word from the right/left

［ðə θə:d fɔ:θ fifθ... wə:d frɔm ðə rait/left］从右/左数第三/四/

五……个词。

the second word /phrase in that last sentence 最后那句话的第二个单

词/短语。

［ðə ˈsekənd wə:d freis in ðæt la:stˈsentəns］

the first/second/last line in the first/second/last paragraph

［ðə fə:stˈsekənd la:st lain in ðə fə:st ˈsekənd la:st ˈpærəgra:f］

第一/二/最后一段的第一/二/最后一行

Situational Dialogic Unit 2

第二情景对话单元

Learn to Speak English

Talking about Majors and Subjects

Helen: You're a student, aren't you?

Xuezi: Yes. But how do you know this, miss?

Helen: As you look very polite and elegant with a pair of spectacles.

Xuezi: You've good eyesight to know what I do.

Helen: Is it so? Please tell me what major you study?

Xuezi: Civil and Industrial Architecture.

Helen: How do you think about your major?

Xuezi: Wonderful! I think. I like it very much.

Helen: Why so, young man?

Xuezi: As you know all the buildings are set up by hard-working and bright builders from ancient times to the present. They're really great. So I'm determined to study architecture after graduation. I'm going to be a builder and build up high buildings and large mansions with my own hands.

Helen: Building millions of apartments for the country and the people, your dream must be realized, young'man. I know you enjoy your major, I believe you must be a top student in your college, and hope you become a builder of benifting people.

Xuezi: Thank you for encouraging. Ours is one of famous architectural college in China. I'm sure to treasure the good chance, study hard and realize my dream.

Helen: I'm glad to hear it. Can you tell me how many majors there're in yours?

Xuezi: Not less than twenty besides Civil and Industrial Architecture, I think.

Helen: Oh, so many. It's worthy of famouse one. And how many subjects are there in your major?

学说英语

谈论专业和课程

海　伦：你是一名学生，对吗？

学　子：对。不过你是怎么知道的，小姐？

海　伦：因为你戴着一副眼镜，温文尔雅。

学　子：您可真有眼力，就连我做什么的都能看出来。

海　伦：是吗？请告诉我你学的什么专业好吗？

学　子：工（业与）民（用）建（筑）。

海　伦：你认为你的专业怎样？

学　子：我认为挺好！我很喜欢。

海　伦：为什么如此喜欢，年轻人？

学　子：正如所知，从古到今所有的建筑物都是由勤劳而又聪明的建筑者们建起来的，他们真伟大！所以我立志学建筑，毕业后就要成为一名建设者，也能亲手建设起高楼大厦。

海　伦：建成广厦千万栋，兴邦利国为人民。你的梦想一定能实现，青年人。我知道你喜爱你的专业，我也相信你一定是你们学校的好学生，更希望你成为一名造福于民的建设者。

学　子：多谢你的鼓励。我们学校是中国最富有名望的建筑院校之一。我一定珍惜这一良机、刻苦学习、实现梦想。

海　伦：我很高兴听到这点。你能告诉我，你们学校有多少个专业吗？

学　子：除了工（业与）民（用）建（筑）专业外，我想不少于20个。

海　伦：啊！这么多，真不愧是一所名校。你的专业设有多少门课程？

Xuezi: More than ten, I suppose. For example: construction materials, architecture of houses, construction technique, construction organization and mechanics, etc. are required course, English and political economy etc. belong to basic course.

Helen: So many subjects. What methods do your teachers usually adopt?

Xuezi: They usually adopt individualized method of instruction, use method of discussion and elicitation and cultivate us the ability to analyze and solve problems independently.

Helen: That's nice. How do they teach you?

Xuezi: They seriously explain the questions from the shallower to the deeper and from the easier to the more advanced, and explaining profound theories in simple language.

Helen: I think it's programmed instruction. By the way, what about your teaching facilities in your college?

Xuezi: Very good. In order to develop our operation skill, we study basic princeples of science in the teaching buildings and learn how to use scientific apparatuses and machinery in the laboratories.

Helen: Integrating theory with practice and doing practice geared to the needs of the job is a new teaching way. Is your college large?

Xuezi: Yes. Very large, two square kilometers or so.

Helen: So large. Would you please show me yours?

Xuezi: OK, follow me, please.

Helen: Oh. Your tidy and neat campouse, tall teaching and office buildings, blocks of flats and laboratories, complete majors, all of necessary facilities are brought up and trained the cradle of modernizing architectural talents.

Xuezi: Yes, it's true for our teachers "Internationally known site of learning and academic research."

学　子：我想有 10 多门吧。例如：建筑材料、房屋建筑学、施工技术、施工组织、力学等多门必修课程，英语和政治经济学等属于基础课。

海　伦：这么多课程。老师们通常采用什么方法教学？

学　子：通常采用因材施教法，运用讨论式和启发式教学法，并培养我们独立分析问题和解决问题的能力。

海　伦：很好么。老师们怎样讲授？

学　子：由浅入深、由易到难，深入浅出地认真讲解。

海　伦：我认为这是循序渐进的教学。顺便问一句，你们学院的教学设施怎样？

学　子：很好。为了提高我们的操作技能，我们在教学大楼里学习基本科学原理，在实验室里学习怎样使用科学仪器和设备。

海　伦：理论联系实际和对口实习是一种新的教学方式。你们的学院很大吗？

学　子：是的，很大，大约 2 平方公里的面积。

海　伦：就那么大！能带我看看你们学校吗？

学　子：好的，请随我来。

海　伦：啊！你们整洁的校园，高大的教学和办公大楼、学生公寓大楼和试验室，专业设置齐全，设施配套是培养和造就现代化建筑人才的摇篮。

学　子：是。对于我们的老师们来说"良师育英才，桃李满天下"这倒是真的。

Formulaic Communication 日常交际习语

Thanks and Responses 感谢与应答

1. Thank you very /so much. 非常感谢您/多谢多谢。

2. Thanks very much indeed. 确实得谢谢。

3. Thanks a lot. 多谢。

4. I'm very sincerely/grateful/obliged to you. 非常/衷心/十分感激您。

5. Thak you for your. . . . 谢谢您的……。

6. It's very kind of you to. . . 为……谢谢你。

7. I'm very gratefull to you for. . . 很感谢你为我……。

1. Oh, no, don't mention it. 啊，不，不值一谢。

2. Not at all. 不必谢。

3. Oh, never mind it, you're quite welcome. 〔美语〕啊，没关系；别客气。

4. At your service. 愿为您效劳。

5. You're very kind. 您太客气了。

6. It's nothing/Think nothing of it. 〔美语〕这不算什么。

7. No trouble at all. 一点也不麻烦。

8. Oh, no, it's a/ with pleasure. 啊，不。那是件乐事/很乐意。

9. It was a pleasure for me. You've/There's nothing to thank me for.
   对我来说这是一件愉快的事。(你）没什么可谢的。

Explanatory Notes注释：

1. 英语中常把两个形容词用 and 连接起来表达一个意思。这两个词互相影响，互相说明和补充。如 clear and cold（凉爽清新），parched and dry（干燥），polite and elegant（温文尔雅），safe and sound（安然无恙），crude and rude（粗野无礼）等。

2. 英语问候用语很多，这里仅列举部分最常用的用语以便在不同场合选择使用：

   1）英语问候用语均为套语，例如：Good-morning. 早上好。（用于午饭前一段时间）只能用 Good-morning. 回答，Good afternoon. 下午好。（用于午饭后到下午五点左右这段时间），Good evening. 晚上好。（用于六点后的时间）也用同样词语来回答对方。

   2）Hello 是美国用语，发［'he'lou］音，Hullo 是英国用语，发［'hʌ'lou］音，语气较随便，所以在特别正式的场合是不能用的。由于 Hello/Hullo 相当于汉语的"喂"之意，因此是口语中经常使用的打招呼用语，不管是熟人还是陌生人之间均可使用，还可用于一天的所有时间。现在人们之间常用更简单的 Hi 代替 Hello/Hullo。

   3）How are you? 意为"你好"，也是一种常用而有不分早晚的问候用语，但这种用语要用固定语来回答才符合英语习惯。

   A. How are you?

   B. Fine/OK/Not too bad，thanks，and you?

   A. Very well. Thank you.

   4）How do you do? 只能用于第一次见面的陌生人之间，意为"您好"，对方也回答"How do you do?"作为相应的致意。
   这是很正式的用语，往往用于较客气的场合，讲这句话时，常伴随着双方互相握手，所以用这样的用语来迎接宾客。

Spoken Practice 口语练习

1. Pair Work：

Suppose you're a student who studies the Construction Management（施工管理）in a University of Architectural Engineering. Try to introduce yourself to the others including your major, objects and others.

2. Tell "true" or "false" in accordance with Learn to Speak English：

1) (　　) Helen studies Civil and Industrial Architecture.

2) (　　) All the buildings are built by hard-working and bright builders from ancient times to present.

3) (　　) There're more than twenty subjects in the major of civil & industrial architecture.

4) (　　) Teachers in our college cultivate student's the ability to analyze and solve problems independently.

5) (　　) Architectural universities cultivate and train the cradle of modernizing architectural talents.

3. Read & Interpret the Following Passage：

Our College

Our college is located in the suburb of the city, not very far from the city. Transportation is convenient and the environment is pleasing. In our college, there are over twenty teaching buildings and blocks of flats, two libraries, several laboratories, an office building, an auditorium, a science building, a gym and a big sports ground. The college constructs a perfect atmosphere for students to study and stay.

4. Learn the Following Usefull Abbreviated Words by Heart：

C. E. = civil engineer　　　　　　　土木工程师

E. E. = electrical engineer　　　　　电气工程师

M. E. = mechnical engineer　　　　　机械工程师

P. E. = professional engineer　　　　专业工程师

C. P. A = Chartered public accountant　注册会计师

P. A. = punchasing agent　　　　　　采购代理人

insp. = inspector 监理

arch. = architect 建筑师

eng. = engineer 工程师

mach. = machinist 机械师

5. Practise Reading the Following. Pay Special Attention to the Loss of Plosion（失去爆破）：

good-bye［ˈgu(d)ˈbai］ blackboard［ˈblæ(k)bɔːd］

doctor［ˈdɔ(k)tə］ grandpa［ˈgræn(d)paː］

sit down［si(t)daun］ take care［tei(k)kɛə］

knock down［nɔ(k)daun］ stop talking［ˈstɔ(p)ˈtɔːkiŋ］

a great deal［ə griː(t)diːl］ a good builder［ə gu(d)ˈbildə］

at that time［ə(t)ðæ(t)taim］ last night［laːs(t)nait］

6. Substitute the Following Words & Expressions：

1）Use the following **Terms about Majors and Subjects（专业和课程相关术语）** to replace the black words in the following sentence：

Helen：Oh, so many. It's worthy of famouse one. And how many **subjects** are there in your **major**?

海　伦：啊! 这么多，真不愧是一所名校。你的**专业**设有多少门**课程**?

Majors and Subjects［ˈmeidʒəz ənd ˈsʌbdʒiktz］专业和课程

architecture［ˈaːkitektʃə］建筑学

engineering machinery［ˌendʒiˈniəriŋ məˈʃiːnəri］工程机械

civil engineering［ˈsivlˌendʒiˈniəriŋ］土木工程

architectural engineering［ˈaːkitektʃərəl ˌendʒiˈniəriŋ］建筑工程

hydraulic engineering［haiˈdrɔːlik ˌendʒiˈniəriŋ］水利工程

architectural economcs［ˈaːkitektʃərəl ˌiːkəˈmɔmiks］建筑经济

electrical installation［iˈlektrikəl ˌinstəˈleiʃən］电气安装

water supply and sewerage［ˈwɔːtə səˈplai ənd ˈsjuəridʒ］给排水

heating and ventilation［ˈhiːtiŋ ənd ˌventiˈleiʃən］供暖与通风

structural mechanics［ˈstrʌktʃərəl miˈkæniks］结构力学

mechanics of materials［miˈkæniks əv məˈtiəriəl］材料力学

engineering mechanics［ˌendʒiˈniəriŋ miˈkæniks］工程力学

architectural mechanics［ˌaːkiˈtektʃərəl miˈkæniks］建筑力学

construction technique［kənˈstrʌkʃən tekˈniːk］施工技术

construction organization［kənˈstrʌkʃən ˌɔːgənaiˈzeiʃən］施工组织

management of enterprises［ˈmænidʒmənt əvˈentəpraizis］企业管理

contract management［ˈkɔntrækt ˈmænidʒmənt］合同管理

construction budget［kənˈstrʌkʃən ˈbʌdʒit］施工预算

construction quota［kənˈstrʌkʃənˈkwoutə］施工定额

engineering cost［ˌendʒiˈniəriŋ kɔst］工程造价

supervision of works［ˌsjuːpəˈviʒən əv wəːks］工程管理

management of materials［ˈmænidʒmənt əv məˈtiəriəlz］材料管理

technological management［ˌteknəˈlɔdʒikəl ˈmænidʒmənt］技术管理

construction survey［kənˈstrʌkʃən səːˈvei］施工测量

building decoration［ˈbildiŋ ˌdekəˈreiʃən］建筑装饰

reading and making drawings［ˈriːdiŋ ənd ˈmeikiŋ ˈdrɔːiŋz］识图与制图

management of quality［ˈmænidʒmənt əv ˈkwɔliti］质量管理

construction accounting［kənˈstrʌkʃən əˈkauntiŋ］建筑企业会计

management accounting［ˈmænidʒmənt əˈkauntiŋ］管理会计

ecomomic management［ˌiːkəˈmɔmik ˈmænidʒmənt］经济管理

labour and wage management［ˈleibə ənd weidʒ ˈmænidʒmənt］劳动工资管理

financial accunting management［faiˈnænʃəl əˈkauntiŋ ˈmænidʒmənt］财务会计管理

management of machinery & equipment［ˈmænidʒmənt əv məˈʃiːnəri ənd iˈkwipmənt］机械设备管理

safety in production management［ˈseifti in prəˈdʌkʃən ˈmænidʒmənt］安全生产管理

2）Use the following **Country，Capital，People and Language**（国家、首都、人民和语言）to replace the black words in the following sentence：

Xuezi：More than ten，I suppose. For example：construction materials， architecture of houses，construction technique，construction organization and mechanics，etc. are required course，**English** and political economy etc. belong to basic course。

学　子：我想有 10 多门吧。例如：建筑材料、房屋建筑学、施工技术、施工组织、力学等多门必修课程，**英语**和政治经济学等是基础课。

Country，Capital，People and Language 国家、首都、人民和语言

Country	Capital	People	Languange
China / P. R. C.	Beijing	Chinese	Chinese
Americ/U. S. A.	Washington D. C.	Amerian	English
Russia	Moscow	Russian	Russian
France/ F. R.	Paris	Frenchman	French
Country	Capital	People	Languange
Germany	Berlin	Germen	German
India /R. I	New delhi	Indian	Hindi
Australia	Canberra	Australian	English
Canada/C. A.	Ottawa	Canadian	English/French
New Zealand	Wellington	New Zealander	English
Britain/U. K.	London	British/ Englishmen	English
Japan	Tokyo	Japanese	Japanese
Spain	Madrid	Spanish	Spanish
Italy	Rome = Roma	Italian	Italian
Egypt	Cairo	Egyptian	Egyptian

Situational Dialogic Unit **3**

第三情景对话单元

Learn to Speak English

Talking about How to Learn English Well

Liuli：Hi, sir. You can speak an idiomatic English, and are you an Englishman or an American?

Jeck：Englishman, naturally colloquial expression is pretty good, youngman. Can I help you?

Liuli：Sure. I'm a Chinese student, and in fact I know English is one of the important subjects in all the schools and I spent a lot of time in and also put too mush energy into studying it but I have often made little or no progress in my studying. Would you please help me to improve myself in English?

Jeck：OK. First of all, you must know the mastery of it is not an easy job, and you may meet with all kinds of difficulties and you must overcome them in your studies.

Liuli：Right. It's so.

Jeck：Second is "practice" in a word. Do you practise it every day?

Liuli：Yes. Sometimes I do.

Jeck：You know that learning a language is like playing a musical instrument. You must work hard and practise it every day. Practice makes perfect. Do you know the Chinese saying means?

Liuli：Yes. Please tell me how to practise it, sir?

Jeck：OK. You should listen hard, when you listen to English in class, on the radio, anywhere, listen hard.

Liuli：I see. But what uses for it?

Jeck：It helps you to get used to the sound—pronunciation, intonation though you may not understand all the words very well.

Liuli：Is it important to listen, professor?

学说英语

谈论怎样学好英语

刘　利：嗨，先生！你能操一口地道的英语，那你是英国人还是美国人？

杰　克：年轻人，我是英国人，口语自然就不错了。能为你效劳吗？

刘　利：当然。我是中国学生，其实我也知道英语是每个学校的重要的学科之一，我在英语学习上花费了大量的时间，也投入很大的精力，但总是收效甚微。请帮我提高我的英语水平好吗？

杰　克：可以。首先你得知道要掌握英语并非是件容易的事，你可能会在学习中遇到各种各样的困难，但一定要克服它们。

刘　利：对，应该这样。

杰　克：第二点就是一个字"练"。你每天都练习英语吗？

刘　利：是的。我有时天天练。

杰　克：你知道，学习语言就像弹奏乐器一样，必须努力学，天天练。你懂得"熟能生巧"的含义吗？

刘　利：懂得。先生请给我指点一下怎样才能练好吗？

杰　克：好。你应认真听，课堂上听、听收音机，无论在什么地方，都要认真听。

刘　利：我明白了，但听有何用处？

杰　克：虽然你不可能听懂所有的词语，但听有助于你熟悉发音——语音和语调。

刘　利：听有那么重要吗，教授？

Jeck: Yes. As a matter of fact, if you can't produce the sounds of a language acceptably, then you can't really hear them when other people make them; On the contrary, if you can't hear the sounds of a language, then you probably can't write the language well.

Liuli: One's inadequate pronunciation contributes to making one's writing substandard, right?

Jeck: That's true enough. The third is reading.

Liuli: How can I read it perfectly, sir?

Jeck: Go outside early in the morning and read your text aloud for a while. If possible, learn them by heart.

Liuli: I remember reading more. But what's the advantage of reading more, please tell me?

Jeck: Too much, for example, practice type of month, changing tong is convience, voice of reading aloud is not true to the original, recide actually accumnulates knowlege.

Liuli: What you said is really fine and be rich in philosophy, I know your meaning. Anything else to point out?

Jeck: Yeah. Speaking. Speaking English is comprehensive showing for studying English. Whenever or wherever you meet your classmates or others, try to talk with them in English.

Liuli: OK. By the way, why is it so important to learn how to spell properly?

Jeck: Because you spell satisfactorily, you're considered as educated person, otherwise you're considered as an uneducated person by other persons (illiteracy).

Liuli: I got the picture. No pains, no gains. I must follow your instruction. Thank you for your advice.

Jeck: You are welcome. In this way, I believe you must get twice the result with half the effort, and can get good achievement in your study and catch up with top students.

Liuli: I wish it were true.

杰　克：有。事实上，对于一种语言如果你不能正确地发音，那么当别人发这些音时，你就不可能听懂。恰恰相反，如果你听不懂一种语言的发音，也许你就不可能很好地书写这种语言。

刘　利：一个人发音不合格会导致他的书写也不能令人满意，对吗？

杰　克：正是。第三点是读。

刘　利：先生，我怎么读才好？

杰　克：清早起来走出户外，大声朗读一会儿课文，如果可能地话，背下来。

刘　利：我记住了要多读。还有什么要指出的吗？

杰　克：说。讲英语是学习英语的综合表现。无论何时何地遇见同学或其他人，尽量用英语同他们交谈。

刘　利：好。顺便问一声，为什么学会准确拼写又如此重要？

杰　克：因为你能准确无误地拼音，人家就会把你看作是受过教育的人。否则在别人眼里你是个缺乏教育的人（文盲）。

刘　利：我清楚了，没有付出就不会有收获。我一定按照你的教诲去做，多谢你的忠告。

杰　克：不客气。采用这种学习方法，我相信你一定能收到事半功倍的效果，会取得好成绩并能赶上顶级学生。

刘　利：但愿如此。

第一部

Formulaic Communication 日常交际习语

Expressing Language Barriers 表达语言障碍

1. Pardon？（用升调）请再说一遍好吗？

2. Would you please say it again/slowly？请你再说一遍/慢一点好吗？

3. What do you mean by saying that? 你说这话是何意？

4. I'm sorry I can't follow you. 抱歉，我没听清你的话。

5. I'm sorry to know a little English. 对不起，我只懂一点点英语。

6. I'm afraid/sorry. I don't understand you at all. 对不起我根本听不懂你讲的话。

7. I can just make myself understood. 我只能使别人听懂我的话。

8. It's so difficult for me to understand when people speak to me. 别人和我会话时，对我说来听力是最大的障碍。

Explanatory Notes注释:

1. Certainly 当然可以（是语气词）。英语在肯定回答时，为了避免总是用 Yes 回答的呆板，完全可以根据回答语气的需要采用多元化的方式和使用不同的词语进行恰当的回答。如：自然可以—Of course，为什么可以—Why certainly，请便好了—Please do，很乐意—With pleasure，请随便—If you please，相当对—Quite so，正是如此—Exactly，绝对是的—Absolutely，正是这样—Precisely，完全正确—Quite right，你说得对—You're right，我认为是这样—I think so，是啊，随意好啦—Yes, if you like，完全可以—By all means，（完全）肯定—（Quite）true，这也是我的意见—That's my opinion, too，这正是我所说/想的 That's just what I say/think，毫无可疑的—There's no doubt about it 等词语来做肯定回答。

2. Thank you for your advice. 多谢你的忠告。

   thank you for 和 thank you to 都是两个很有用短语，但其用法是有区别的，thank you for + n./v + ing 句型用于事情发生后，与 will 连用表示请求与要求。如：Thank you for your help/helping. 谢谢您的帮助。I will thank you for a cup of tea. 请给我一杯茶。thank you to + v. 句型则用于事情发生前，与 will 连用表示请求与责备。如：I will thank you to come at eight. 请六点钟来。

Spoken Practice口语练习

1. Pair Work：

A is a student. B is a teacher of English. A's English is poor, so A wants to improve him/herself in English.. A meets B and asks B how to study English well. Try to say what instruction and suggestion B gives A.

2. Tell "true" or "false" in accordance with Learn to Speak English：

1）（　　）I spend a lot of time in studying English but I have made much progress in my studying.

2）（　　）Studying English like playing musical instruments must work hard and practised every day.

3）（　　）Everyone must listen to English hard wherever so as to get used to the sound.

4）（　　）Reading more is very important for every student to study English.

5）（　　）Studying English is comprehensive showing for speaking English.

3. Read & Interpret the Following Passage：

Differences between American and British English

Perhaps many people don't know the following three differences between American and British English：

1）Spelling difference. For example, the words in British English are spelt colour、centre and travelled, but these in American English are spelt color, center and traveled.

2）Pronouncing difference. For instance, Americans say dance [dæns], not [nat], hurry ['hə：ri] however Englishmen say dance [da：ns], not [nɔt], hurry ['hʌri].

3）Difference of Using words and expressions. For example, Americans use gas, mail, right away, I guess and so on but people in British use petrol, post, at once, I think.

4. Give the Following Liaison Marks（连读符号⌣）and Try to read Them with Liaison（连读）：

Stand up ［stænd ʌp］　　　　　Come in ［kʌm in］

Thank you ［θæŋ k ju］　　　　first of all ［fə:st əv ɔ:l］

not at all ［nɔt ət ɔ:l］　　　　in an hour ［in ən ' auə］

one of our own ［wʌn əv'auər əun］　in an instant ［in ən 'instənt］

pick it up ［pik it ʌp］　　　　Here it is ［hiər it iz］

Take it away ［teik it ə'wei］　　more and more ［mɔr ənd mɔ］

Take a look at it ［teik ə luk ət it］　here and there ［'hiər ənd θɛə］

5. Learn the Following Usefull Abbreviated Words by Heart：

const. = construction　　　施工，建造

inst. = installation　　　　安装

mg. = managcment　　　　管理，经营

econ. = economy　　　　　经济

pro. = production　　　　　生产

proj. = project　　　　　　计划，工程

est. = estimate　　　　　　预算，估价

G. B. A = gross building area　总建筑占地面积

T. M. = technical manual　　技术手册/指南

6. Substitute the Following Words & Expressions：

1) Use the following **Terms about Written Translation**（笔译相关术语）to replace the black words in the following sentence：

Jeck：Second is "practice" in a word. Do you **practise** it every day?

杰　克：第二点就是一个字"练"。你每天都**练习**英语吗?

Terms about Written Translation ［tə:ms ə'baut'ritn͵træns'leitʃən］

笔译相关术语

expression ［iks'preʃən］习惯表达法

understand ［͵ʌndə'stænd］懂得，理解

write a letter ［rait ə'letə］写封信

spell the word ［spel ðə wə:dz］拼写单词

word meaning ［wə:d 'mi:niŋ］单词意思

letter ［'letə］字母

synonym ［'sinənim］同义词

antonym ［'æntənim］反义词

homonym ［'hɔmənim］同音词

homophone ［'hɔməfəun］同音异义词

prefix ［'pri：fiks］前缀

suffix ［'sʌfiks］后缀

2）Use the following **Comparison between British and American Spelling**（英美惯用拼写对照）to replace the black words in the following sentence：

Liuli：OK. By the way，why is it so important to learn how to **spell** properly?

刘　利：好。顺便问一声，为什么学会准确**拼写**又如此重要？

Comparison between British and American Spelling
英美惯用拼写对照

英语	美语	（英-美）例词／发音	汉语词意
-que	-ck	cheque——check ［tʃek］	支票
-tte	-t	cigarette——cigarete ［ˌsigə'ret］	香烟，纸烟
en-	in-	enquire——inquire ［in'kwaiə］	询问
-ce	-se	vice——vise ［vais］	（老）虎钳
-s-	-z-	cosy——cozy ［'kouzi］	舒适的
-our	-or	colour——color ［'kʌlə］	色彩，颜料
-ph-	-f-	sulphur——sulfur ［'sʌfə］	硫磺
-gue	-g	catalogue——catalog ［'kætələg］	目录
-ll-	-l-	jewellery——jewelry ［'dʒu：əlri］	珠宝
-re	-er	metre——meter ［'mi：tə］	仪表
-y-	-i-	flyer——flier ［'flaiə］	飞行物
-ou-	-o-	fount——font ［faunt］	喷泉
-gg-	-g-	waggon——wagon ［'wægən］	货车
-ise	-ize	organise——organize ［'ɔ：gənaiz］	组织

续表

英语	美语	（英-美）例词／发音	汉语词意
-ar	-er	pedlar——pedler［ˈpedlə］	货郎，小商贩
-xion	-ction	connexion——connection［kəˈnekʃən］	连接
-l-	-ll-	fulfill——fulfil［fulˈfil］	完成
-mm	-m	kilogramm——kilogram［ˈkiləgræm］	公斤
-e-	（e 省略）	adjustement——adjustment［əˈdʒʌstmənt］	调整，调节

【注】英美惯用拼写对照是用具体词例说明拼写上的不同，以消除在实际应用中因缺少这方面的知识而把错误的拼写误认为正确的拼写，反之把正确的拼写误认为错误的拼写，却放过了真正拼写错误或把已学过的单词因拼写不同而误认为是生词造成理解上的偏差和误解。

Situational Dialogic Unit 4

第四情景对话单元

Learn to Speak English

Talking about Working Language——English

Frank: Can you speak English, young man?

Lingli: Yes, a little, but not too much, sir.

Frank: Never mind. But what's your native language, Chinese or Japanese?

Lingli: I'm a Chinese. Naturally, I speak Chinese. What languages do you know besides English, sir?

Frank: Only English. Do you understand what I said?

Lingli: Yes. Perfectly, as your speaking speed is moderate, but it's very difficult for me to speak it, so it seems stiff, not nature.

Frank: Not bad, I think. Anything in the world is the same and has a process from uncustom to custom. You can speak a little slower at first. After a considerable period of time, you're getting better and better. I think it's meaning of Practice makes perfect, correct?

Lingli: Correct. What you said is true. I've studied English more than three years, I found English is so difficult to study.

Frank: Difficulty is the opposite of easy. How difficult a language is to depend mostly on how much it resembles your own language.

Lingli: I don't understand, sir. What's your meaning?

Frank: That's to say, Chinese and English are complete different family of languages. Chinese is a squared type of writing, but English is alphabetic system of writing. There's no inevitale link between them at all.

Lingli: Yes. You're right.

Frank: Japanese, to some extent, is similar to Chinese. As so many Chinese words in Japanese have been adopted. It's quite easier to learn it. However, if you study diligence in good speaking situation, study it hard and you must improved it quickly.

Lingli: You're right. But you speak English with American accent. Can you repeat what you said?

学说英语

谈论工作用语——英语

弗兰克：年轻人，你会讲英语吗？

伶　俐：是的，先生，会讲一点，但不多。

弗兰克：没关系。那你的母语是什么语种，汉语还是日语？

伶　俐：我是中国人，自然讲汉语。除了英语，你还懂那几种语言，先生？

弗兰克：只懂英语。你能听懂我讲的话吗？

伶　俐：能，完全能听懂，因为你的语速适中。但我说英语却很困难，因此听起来有点儿生硬，不自然。

弗兰克：我觉得还不错。世界上任何事情都有个过程，从不自然到自然。你起初可以先慢一点说，天长日久你就会越说越好。我想这就是熟能生巧的含义，对吧？

伶　俐：对。你说得有道理。我已学了三年多英语，我觉得英语可真难学。

弗兰克：难和易是相对而言的，因为一种语言是否难学，主要看它在多大程度上和你的母语相近。

伶　俐：先生，我不明白，此话怎讲？

弗兰克：也就是说汉语和英语是两种截然不同的语系，汉语是方块文字，而英语却是拼音文字，两种语言根本没有必然的联系。

伶　俐：对。你说的没错。

弗兰克：再说日语和汉语在某种程度上却很相似，由于日语中使用了许多汉字，学起来相对容易些。然而对于学英语而言，如在较好的语言环境中，加之刻苦学，进步一定会很快。

伶　俐：说得对。不过你讲英语带有美语口音。你能把你说的话重复一遍吗？

Frank: OK. I' m an American. Do you know how to pronounce the word "building"? And what's the meaning?

Lingli: Let me think. Oh, it's pronounced ['bildiŋ] and the meaning is big and high house.

Frank: Quite good. English is that our construction contract stipulates working language, all the supervisors and engineering and technical personnel working on this project should not only be able to read and use the technical specifications but also speak it well.

Lingli: I know this. As English is commonly used language and almost two third people in the world can speak it.

Frank: Yes. And how do your fellows know it?

Lingli: Most of them are poor, I think.

Frank: It's not conformed to the rules, and it must bring much trouble and inconvenience in your future work. Hope you put more effort to train your staff.

Lingli: That's my opinion, too.

Frank: You should do your best to train well so as to reach to requirement of contract as early as possible.

Lingli: Yes, except those staff, but general foreman, Mr. Huang can speak English fluently, read and write it well, too.

Frank: OK. Let's go to meet him and talk with him, shall we?

Lingli: All right, sir. I'm going to look for him.

Frank: Thank you. That's very kind of you. (After a while) Have you found him?

Lingli: Sorry, I looked for him everywhere but I couldn't find him yet.

Frank: It's nothing at all. We'll have a chat with him if we have another chance.

弗兰克：可以。我是美国人。"建筑"这个单词怎样读音？其意思又
　　　　是什么？

伶　俐：让我想一想，嗬，读［ˈbildiŋ］音，其意思是"建筑物"。

弗兰克：很好。英语是施工合同规定的工作用语，在这个项目中工作
　　　　的所有的监理，工程师和技术人员不仅要能看懂英文并使用
　　　　英语的技术规范，而且还必须说好英语。

伶　俐：我知道这点，因为英语是世界通用语言，几乎世界上有三分
　　　　之二的人都说英语。

弗兰克：是啊。你们的工友们英语会话水平怎么样？

伶　俐：我想他们的大多数水平却很差。

弗兰克：这可不符合合同规定，也一定会给今后的工作带来很多麻烦
　　　　和不便，你们应加强这方面的培训工作才对。

伶　俐：这也是我的意见。

弗兰克：你们要加大这方面的培训工作，争取尽早达到合同规定。

伶　俐：是。除此外，不过总工长，黄先生能流利地讲英语，读、写
　　　　也都挺不错。

弗兰克：那好，咱们去会会他，和他聊一聊，好不好？

伶　俐：好吧，先生。我这就去找他。

弗兰克：谢谢，太好啦。（过了一会儿）找到了吗？

伶　俐：抱歉，我到处找，但都未找到。

弗兰克：没什么。有机会再聊。

第
一
部

Formulaic Communication 日常交际习语

Spelling Difficulties and Expressing Phonetic Troubles
拼写困难和语音表达障碍

1. How do you pronounce this word? 这个字怎么发（读）音？

2. I can't quite catch the pronunciation of this word.
   我还不大听懂这个字的发音。

3. Can you write it in phonetic characters for me?
   你能否把这个字的音标给我写出来看看？

4. Where's the stress? Is that right? Please listen.
   这个词的重音在哪儿？这样读对吗？请听。

5. How do spell the word? 怎么拼写这个词？

6. Is it used in actual speech? Or is it only a bookship expression.
   这个词能用于实际语言中吗？还仅仅是个书面用语？

7. What does that word mean/What's the meaning of that word?
   这个字是什么意思？

8. Is there any other way of saying it? 这句话还有其他意思吗？

9. This book is beyond me = This book is too difficult for me to read.
   这部书太难了，我看不懂。

Explanatory Notes注释：

1. Yes, except those staff, but general foreman, Mr. Huang can speak English fluently, read and write it well, too. 句中的 except... （除……外）可与 but 通用，但 except 比 but 的意味明确。Except 和 but 用在"除……外"的意思上，通常还和 all、every、any、none 等不定代词并用。而 besides "除……外"（还有）却是用在"附加"的意思上的。它常和 some、many、a few 以及其他分量词连用。试比较：

All went to worksite except him. 除了他外，全体职工都到工地上班了。（意味只有他一人缺勤，其余都到工地上班了。）

All went to worksite besides him. 除了他到工地上班了外，全体职工也都去都到工地上班了。（意味着他自己也在内一同都到工地上班了。）

2. I looked for him everywhere but I couldn't find him yet. 我到处找，但都未找到。句中用了 look for 和 find 两个英语单词却表达了同一个汉语"找"字。能否只用一个？能否把两个单词调换位子？回答都是否定的。这是因为汉语同一个意思的字在英语却有两个或几个词表示其意。这儿一个词强调动作，另一个则强调状态，强调动作的词不能用于表示状态，相反强调状态的词也不能用作表示动作，这就是英汉两种语言的不同之处，应引起高度注意，所以也很有必要再列出部分这类词以便今后选择使用。

listen（to）倾听↔hear 听见　　　look at 看↔see 看到

look for 寻找↔find 找到　　　advise 劝说↔persuade 说服

put on/dress/throw on 穿上↔have on 穿着

try to + v. 努力去做↔manage to + v. 设法做成

Spoken Practice口语练习

1. Pair Work：

Suppose you're students of A Construction technical College and practise on a construction site. Try to talk with the building engineering and technical personnel in English what you see and hear on the busy site.

2. Tell "true" or "false" in accordance with Learn to Speak English：

1）（   ）I can speak little English, especially major English.

2）（   ）My native language is Japanese not Chinese.

3）（   ）Please repeat what you said because I don't understand you.

4）（   ）If your company constructs abroad, English must be the contract working language.

5）（   ）The construction contract requires all the persons on the project should not only be able to read and use the English but also speak it well.

3. Read & Interpret the Following Passage：

How to Learn English Well

To learn a language well, one must know its grammar almost completely, not just its vocabulary or its sounds, not even sets of rules for constructing sentences. But one can't learn a language by studying its grammar. If you do this, you may learn only the grammar and not the language. Instead, by memorizing a great many sentences and learning how to use them, one can learn both the grammar and the language.

4. Practise Reading the Following and Mark the Necessary Liaison (⌣) before Reading Them：

1）Make up your mind. ［meik ʌp jɔːmaind］

2）Come back in a minite. ［kʌm bæk in əˈminit］

3）Here is a huge building. ［hiər iz ə hjuːdʒ ˈbildiŋ］

4）Is it a large city? ［iz it ə laːdʒ ˈsiti］

5）That is our worksite. ［ðæt iz ˈauə ˈwəːksait］

6）Turn on the light. ［təːn ɔn ðə lait］

7）Say it in English. ［sei it in ˈiŋgliʃ］

8）There are many houses along both sides of the street. ［ðɛɑː reɑ əˈmani ˈhausiz əˈlɔŋ bənθ saidz əv ə striːt］

9）There is an English story book on my desk. ［ðɛɑ iz ən iŋgliʃ stɔːri buk ɔn mai desk］

10）Will it take a lot of time to go to town on foot? ［wil it teik ə lɔt əv taim tə gəu tə taun ɔn fut］

5. Learn the Following Usefull Abbreviated Words by Heart：

Dr. （doctor）博士   M.（master）硕士

B.（bachelor）学士   Mr.（Mister）先生

Mrs.（Mistress）夫人   Mr.（Miss）女士

V. O. C.（Voice of China）中国之声

V. O. A.（Voice of America）美国之音

B. B. C.（British Broadcast Corporation）英国广播公司

EPT（English Proficiency Test）英语水平测试

TOEFL ［ˈtoufl］（Test of English As A Foreign Language）托福考试

6. Substitute the Following Words & Expressions：

1）Use the following **Terms about Spoken Language（口语相关术语）** to replace the black words in the following sentence：

Lingli：Yes. Perfectly, as your **speaking speed** is moderate, but it's very difficult for me to **speak** it , so it seems stiff, not nature.

伶　俐：能，完全能听懂，因为你的**语速**适中。但我说英语却很困难。因此听起来有点儿生硬，不自然。

Terms of Spoken Language ［təːmz əv ˈspəukən ˈlæŋgwidʒ］口语术语

interpret ［inˈtəːprit］口译，翻译

speak English ［spiːk ˈiŋgliʃ］讲英语

say ［sei］说（话）

retell ［ˈriːtel］复述，重述

read book ［riːd buk］读/念/看书

repeat ［riˈpiːt］重说

explain ［iksˈplein］解释

native/foreign language ［ˈneitiv ˈfɔrin ˈlæŋgwidʒ］母/外语

49

oral English〔'iŋgliʃ 'ɔːrəl〕英语口语

American accent〔ə'merikən 'æksənt〕美国口音

Shanghai dialect〔shanghai 'daiəlekt〕上海方言

pet phrase〔pet freiz〕口头禅，口头语

the sound of voices〔ðə saund əv 'vɔisiz〕说话声音

eloquence〔'eləkwəns〕口才

short/long vowel〔ʃɔːt lɔŋ 'vauə〕短/长元音

open/close syllable〔'oupən klouz 'siləbl〕开/闭音节

falling/rising/level tone〔'fɔːliŋ 'raiziŋ 'levl toun〕升/降/平调

primary/secondary stress〔'praiməri 'sekəndəri stres〕主/次要重读

phonetic rules〔fou'netik ruːlz〕读音规则

stress mark〔stres maːk〕重读记号

stressed/unstressed syllable〔'strest 'ʌn 'strest 'siləbl〕重/非重读音节

2）Use the following **Comparison between British and American Pro-nunciations**（英美发音对照）to replace the black words in the fol-lowing sentence：

Lingli：Right. But you speak English with **American accent.** Can you repeat what you said?

伶　俐：说得对。不过你讲英语带有**美语口音**。你能把你说的话重复一遍吗？

Comparison between British and American Pronunciations
英美发音对照

音　标		注		音	
英语	美语	例词	词意	英语	美语
〔ɔ〕	〔a〕	dollar	（货币）元	〔'dɔlə〕	〔'dalər〕
		shop	商店	〔ʃɔp〕	〔ʃap〕
〔ɔ〕	〔ɔː〕	dog	狗	〔dɔg〕	〔dɔːg〕
		moth	蛀虫	〔mɔθ〕	〔mɔːθ〕
〔ɔː〕	〔oː〕	orient	东方	〔'ɔːriənt〕	〔'oːriənt〕
		editorial	编辑的	〔ˌedi'tɔːriəl〕	〔ˌedi'toːriəl〕

续表

音 标		注		音	
英语	美语	例词	词意	英语	美语
[a:]	[æ]	glass	玻璃	[gla:s]	[glæs]
		can't	不能	[ka:nt]	[kænt]
[ai]	[i]	agile	敏捷的	['ædʒail]	['ædʒil]
		fragile	易碎的	['frædʒail]	'frædʒil
[ju:]	[u:]	duly	按时地	['dju:li]	['du:li]
		nuclear	核心的	['nju:kliə]	['nu:kliər]
[ʌr]	[ə:r]	hurry	匆忙	['hʌri]	['hə:ri]
		worry	使烦恼	['wʌri]	['wə:ri]
[uər]	[ur]	curious	好奇的	['kjuəriəs]	['kjuriəs]
		assurance	把握	[ə'ʃuərəns]	[ə'ʃurəns]
[iər]	[i(:)r]	hero	英雄	['hiərou]	['hi:rɔ]
		appearance	出现	[ə'piərəns]	[ə'pirəns]
[ou]	[ɔ]	process	工序	['prouses]	['prɔses]
		progress	进步	['prougres]	['prɔgres]

【注】英美发音不同是英美英语不同之一，这一点有必要对初学者说明，否则会造成发音上的误解。为了确保正确的发音，口语练习中列出了英美发音对照表，其目的就是让读者详细了解并切实注意其不同之处，以确保今后口语会话，特别是听力水平的提高。

第一部

Situational Dialogic Unit 5

第五情景对话单元

Learn to Speak English

Talking about English Conversation Technique

Mark: Excuse me. Could you tell me why speaking ways between Chinese and Westerner aren't same, to some extent, Ms?

Juliet: Because both of them have different traditonal culture and life custom, I think.

Mark: I don't understand yet. Would you give me some examples if you don't mind?

Juliet: Never mind. When starting up a conversation, attracting attention, interrupting politely, asking for repetition and asking a favour, the Westerners usually use the expressions like "excuse me", "sorry", "pardon" etc.

Mark: I know if we use these, Westerners are sure to understand what we mean. But how do you make sure someone has got it?

Juliet: The question is quite simple, you can ask "Is that clear?" "Are you still with me?" "Do you understand?" etc. in order to confirm.

Mark: You can only adopt this way to make sure, right?

Juliet: No. You can adopt "I don't know if I make myself clear?" "If there's anything you don't understand, please say so." ask in retort.

Mark: How do you make sure that you have been understood?

Juliet: You can also say "sorry, I'm not quite with you/what you've just said. Do you mean...?" "Is that correct/right?" "Is that what you wanted/said?"....

Mark: Do you have any important points to attend besides these?

Juliet: Yes of course. There're three points, I suppose.

Mark: What's the first, miss?

Juliet: Inspiring somebody to talk. For example: "Who'd like to start/begin You're looking skeptically, what have you got to say?" "What's your opinions on that?" "What do you think?" "Don't you agree?" etc. to be guided.

学说英语

谈论英语会话技巧

马　克：对不起，女士。你能告诉我为什么中国人和西方人说话方式在某种程度上有所不同？

朱丽叶：我认为这是由于传统文化和生活习惯不同而形成的。

马　克：我还有点儿不大明白。如果你不介意的话，给我举些例子好吗？

朱丽叶：没什么。当开场白、引人注意、客气地打断别人、要求重复以及求助时，西方人通常使用"对不起"、"抱歉"、"原谅"等词语。

马　克：我知道假如我们在讲话时使用了这些词语，西方人肯定会明白我们所说的意思。但怎样才能确定对方是否明白你的意图呢？

朱丽叶：这一问题比较简单。为了确定你被理解，你可以询问"这点清楚了吗？""你听得懂吗？""理解了吗？"等来加以证实。

马　克：仅仅采用这些方式就能肯定你被理解了，对吗？

朱丽叶：不对。你还可以采用"不知我是否讲清楚了？""如果你有什么不明白，请提出来。"来反问。

马　克：怎样确定你是否理解对方了？

朱丽叶：你同样可以说"抱歉，我不懂你的话/你刚说的话/你的意思是……？""这就对了吗？""这是你所说/想要的吗？""这话的意思是……？"来证实其意。

马　克：除此之外，还有哪些要点得以注意的吗？

朱丽叶：当然有。我认为还有三点必须注意。

马　克：女士，第一点是什么？

朱丽叶：启发人说话。例如，"谁愿意打头炮？""你看上去还有些怀疑，你想说什么吗？""对于这个问题你有什么看法？""你不赞成吗？"等加以诱导。

Mark: Don't be awkward silence at the situation and bring in other people. What's your second?

Juliet: Summing up. That means "to cut a long story short", "to put the whole thing in a nutshell", "all in all", "so what it comes down to be. . . etc." to be applied.

Mark: Conclude the main idea and stress the main point. I'm interested in the last one, tell me, please.

Juliet: No problem. The last point is terminating a conversation.

Mark: Please give me some examples about this point, OK?

Juliet: OK. For instance, "It's very nice to talk with you, but I'm afraid I can't stay any longer." "I'm awfully sorry, but I'm meeting somebody in two minutes." and even "Well, talk to you later, then." "I'm afraid we'll have to leave it there." "I hope you'll forgive me but I really have to be going." etc. tactfully terminating conversation.

Mark: Well, so many for that. Why should we use such kinds of terminating expressions?

Juliet: Because this point is as more important as above.

Mark: What will be taken place if we don't use these expressions or stop talking suddenly?

Juliet: Maybe there're some misunderstanding or make the other side unhappy, and interfere with the whole conversation effect.

Mark: Oh. What you explained is very nice. I gain much in yours. There're so many things for us to pay great attention.

Juliet: Yes, in additions to these, you have to introduce a new point and illustrate a point and even show you are listening while you're doing so.

Mark: I must remember these.

Juliet: Above-mentioned techniques are universally applicable in the Communications of medium coloquialism, meanwhile we've to control our talking. intonation and manner of speaking so as to coordinate our skill.

Mark: What you explained is well presented. You're worthy of educator.

马　克：就是不要冷了场面，让别人发表自己的看法。第二点呢？

朱丽叶：总结。其意是"长话短说"、"总而言之"、"总的来说"、"那归根到底就是……"等词语的应用。

马　克：其实就是概括大意，突出会话要点。我对最后一点也很感兴趣，请给我讲讲吧。

朱丽叶：没问题。最后一点就是结束谈话。

马　克：请给我列举几个实例，好吗？

朱丽叶：好吧。例如，"和你交谈很高兴，但是恐怕我不能再长谈下去了。""非常抱歉，我两分钟后要见一个人。""好吧，回头再谈。""恐怕，我们只能到此为止了。""希望你能原谅我，我真的该走了。"等婉转地终止会话。

马　克：啊，那么多的方式结束会话。为什么应该使用这些用语呢？

朱丽叶：因为这一点和以上几点同样重要。

马　克：如果不用这些套语就终止谈话会怎样？

朱丽叶：突然终止谈话，可能会造成一些误解或使对方不快，以影响整个谈话效果。

马　克：啊，你讲的真好，我受益匪浅。有这么多事项需要我们引起高度注意。

朱丽叶：是的。除此之外，你在会话期间，还得注意不断地引入新话题、说明观点甚至于表明你在倾听对方。

马　克：我一定记住这些。

朱丽叶：以上所讲的只适用于中性语体的交际场合，同时还得掌握好谈话的语调和语气，以配合好其技巧的运用。

马　克：你讲的有板有眼，真不愧是位教育专家。

Formulaic Communication 日常交际习语

Expression of Hearing Troubles 表达听力障碍

1. I didn't catch what you said. 我没听懂你的话。

2. I don't quite know what you call it? 我不知道你把他叫什么?

3. I think you must know what I mean. 我想你懂了我的意思。

4. I can't think of an exact word, but you know.

   我再也找不出合适的字眼来，但你是懂我的意思的。

5. Most foreigners speak English too quickly to be understood.

   大多数外国人讲话都太快听不懂。

6. I can understand fairly well if you speak slowly.

   假如你讲慢点，我会明白你的意思。

Explanatory Notes注释：

1. 在回答对方问题时，如需要使用表示否定意思时应特别注意，否则会使对方不悦或发怒，直接影响到对方的感情和会话效果。值得一提的是，有些否定用语的语气比较强，例如：Certainly not. （不一定是。），Impossible. （不可能。），Of course not. （当然不。）和 You must be mistaken. （你一定搞错了吧。）等一定要注意场合慎重使用。为了使表达否定或异议的语气有所减弱，就必须使用一些套语。例如：Oh, ... （哦……）；Personally, ... （就我个人而言，……）；Well, … （这个，……）；As I see it, ... （我认为……）；I would say... （我愿说……）；but don't you think...？（但您不认为……?）；To tell truth, ... （老实说，……）；There's something in what you say, but... （您说的话有点道理，但是……）；Oh, I don't know. It seems to me that..., （哦，我不知道。好像……,）；As a matter of fact, ... （事实上，……）等。

2. 英美人的姓名（full name），名在前姓在后，这点完全不同于中国人的姓在前名在后的习惯。从位置先后可分为 first name 名和 last name 姓（美国英语）。（英国英语）名是 given name；姓为 family name/surname，两者之间若有中间名 middle name，中间名则多用简写。如：

名	中间名	姓
given name	middle name/Christian name	family name/surname
John	F. / Fitsgerald	Kennedy

3. 英美男人和女人还有全称，简称和爱称/昵称（中国人叫小名）。

如：全称	简称	爱称/昵称
John（约翰）	Jack（贾克）	Johnny（约翰尼）
Katherine（凯瑟琳）	Kate（凯特）	Katie（凯蒂）

Spoken Practice 口语练习

1. Pair Work：

Supposing A acts as a professor of English. B acts as a college student who wants to consult A what conversation techniques B should adopt and what B should control while talking.

2. Answer the following questions in accordance with Learn to Speak English：

1) (　　) What should you say if you start up a conversation, interrupt politly, ask for repetition or even attract attention?

2) (　　) How can you make sure that you have been understood?

3) (　　) Are you sure of success if you control above-mentioned conversation techniques? Why?

4) (　　) What main techniques must you use during your conversation in order to realize your aim?

5) (　　) What do you pay attention to besides the conversation techniques in **Learn to Speak English**?

3. Read & Interpret the Following Passage：

Commmon International Language—English

English is one of commmonly used international languages. According to the statistical figures in 1986, people used English as their native language are more than four hundred million. Nearly one fifth population of the world, to some extent, speak English including people in U. K, U. S. A, Canada, New Zealand and Australia. In addition to, English is used as official language and their second language is more than twenty coutries.

According to using English limits of the world, 70% posts and broardcasts, most documents of science and technology, most conferences are all adopted English as commmonly used first international language. Naturally, English is one of official working languages in the U. N.

4. Practise Reading the Following Sentences with the Correct Intonation according to the Marks of Falling or rising tone：

1）Do you have a new computer in your ↗ office? No，I ↘ don't.

2）There are so many beautiful houses in the ↘ compus，aren't ↗ there?

3）Do you speak ↗ English or ↘ France?

4）Are there any constructors on your ↗ worksite? Yes，there ↘ are.

5）We learn ↗ English，↗ computer，construction ↗ budget，ecomomic ↗ management，management of ↗ enterprises and other ↘ subjects in our college.

5. Learn the Following Words by Heart and Pay Attention to the Changing Forms：

abbr. —reference	abbr. —reference	abbr. —reference
Length	**Weight**	**Capacity**
km. -kilometre	kg. -kilogram（me）	kl. -kilolitre
m. -metre	g. -gram（me）	l. -litre
cm. -centimetre	cg. -centigram（me）	cl. -centilitre
mm. -millimeter	mg. -milligram（me）	ml. -millilitre
in. -inch	ft. -foot/feet	

6. Substitute the Following Words & Expressions：

1）Use the following **Terms about Grammar（语法相关术语）** to replace the black words in the following sentence:

Mark：Oh，there're so many **idioms** for us to **pay great attention.**

马　克：啊，有这么多习语需要我们注意。

Terms about Grammar ［tɔːmz əˈbaut ˈgræmə］语法相关术语

simple sentence ［ˈsimpl ˈsentəns］简单句

noun phrase ［naun freiz］名词短语

verb idiom ［vəb ˈidiəm］成语动词

dictionary ［ˈdikʃənəri］英语词典

English grammar ［ˈiŋgliʃ ˈgræmə］英语语法

mistakes in grammar ［misˈteik in ˈgræmə］语法错误

grammatical analysis ［grəˈmætikəl əˈnæləsis］语法分析

2）Use the following **Some idiomatic Expressions in English（一些英语习惯表达方式）** to replace the black words in the following sentence：

Juliet：Summing up. That means **"to cut a long story short"**, **"to put the whole thing in a nutshell"**, **"all in all"**, **"so what it comes down to be...etc."** to be applied.

朱丽叶：总结。其意是**"长话短说"**、**"总而言之"**、**"总的来说"**、**"那归根到底就是……"** 等词语的应用。

Some idiomatic Expressions in English [sʌm ˌidiəˈmætik iksˈpreʃənz in ˈiŋliʃ] 一些英语习惯表达方式

She's my namesake. [ʃiz mai ˈneimseik] 她和我同姓/名。

He's letting me down. [hiz ˈletiŋ mi：daun] 他使我失望。

She doesn't care. [ʃi ˈdʌznt kɛə] 她满不在乎。

He knows what he is doing. [hi nouz hwɔt hiz ˈduːiŋ] 他很内行。

That's what I'm driving at. [ðætz hwɔt aim ˈdraiviŋ ət] 这就是我的意思。

How right you are! [hau rait ju aː] 你说的完全正确。

That's where it is. [ðætz hwɛə it iz] 这话说到节骨眼上。

Don't jump to conclusions. [dount dʒʌmp tu kənˈkluʒən] 别武断地下结论。

There's something in what you say. [ðɛəz ˈsʌmθiŋ in hwɔt ju sei] 你说的有些道理。

You have hit the nail on the head. [ju hæv hit ðə neil ɔn ðə hed] 你真是一语道破。

We don't speak the same language. [wi dount spiːk ðə seim ˈlæŋgwidʒ] 我们没有共同语言。

Situational Dialogic Unit **6**

第六情景对话单元

Learn to Speak English

Talking about Interviewing for a Job

Knox: You're welcome, miss, please sit down.

Hujie: Thank you, sir. Please call me Hujie.

Knox: OK. Hujie. I'd like to enquire about your qualification. Which architectural university were you graduated from?

Hujie: American University of Architectural Science & Technology。

Knox: Good one, famous one in the world. But what major did you study?

Hujie: Civil and Industrial Architecture. This major of the educational system is four years. I got English Proficiency Test (EPT), Test of English as a foreign Languauge (TOEFL), I made good grades and obtain scholar degree.

Knox: I see. Please show me your documents, OK?

Hujie: Certainly. That's just what I think. Here you are. This is my resume, application form and papers, please check and appove.

Knox: Let me read it. Our group-corporation is a state-owned enterprise, as requirement of production development, we need to inlarge our team of engineering and technical personnel. What would you like to take up as career in the posts?

Hujie: A civil engineer, I think. It's my aspiration.

Knox: Fine. Which would you rather go in for, inside work or outside one?

Hujie: As you know, I'm just graduated and only have some book knowlege, but lack of practical working experience. So it's better for me to work on the site so as to study for the purpose of application and improve my practical working ability.

Knox: I know what you mean. We pay the salary according to the post. That is to say, the post decides payment. You'll bea technician first, the salary is 1,000-1,500 per month, I suppose.

Hujie: I know the salary already. Would you please tell me other things about this job?

学说英语

谈论求职面试

诺克斯：欢迎你，小姐，请坐。

胡　洁：谢谢，先生。请叫我胡洁吧。

诺克斯：好吧，胡洁。我想先询问你的资格。你毕业于哪所建筑大学？

胡　洁：美国建筑科技大学。

诺克斯：好学校、世界名校。那你学什么专业？

胡　洁：工（业与）民（用）建（筑）。这个专业的学制是四年，我通过了英语水平测试、托福考试，我的成绩很好，并获得学士学位。

诺克斯：我明白了。请给我看看你的相关证件好吗？

胡　洁：当然可以！这正是我所想的，请看吧。这是我的简历、申请表和相关证件，请审阅。

诺克斯：我看一看。我们集团公司是一家国营企业，由于生产发展的需要，要扩大工程技术人员队伍。你想从事这种职业的哪一岗位？

胡　洁：我想成为一名土木工程师，这是我的志向。

诺克斯：很好。你更希望搞什么工作，室内工作还是室外工作？

胡　洁：你知道我刚刚毕业，只有书本知识，缺乏实际经验，所以最好在现场工作，以便学以致用，提高我实际的工作能力。

诺克斯：我明白你的意思。我们是依岗定薪，也就是说，岗位决定薪水。我想聘你当技术员，月薪是 1000～1500 元。

胡　洁：薪水我已知道。你能告诉我一些其他相关的事吗？

Knox: OK. For instance: We pay a bonus twice a year and give three week holidays a year, working hours begin at nine A. M. and finish at five P. M., we work a five-day work.

Hujie: I see. Would you mind telling me how long you review my salary?

Knox: Usually six months later. Do you have any questions about this job?

Hujie: Yeah. I'd like to know whether there's a retirement plan, pension scheme and medical insurance?

Knox: Naturally. Ours runs by state, we do everything according to regulations of our state.

Hujie: I suppose this is important for an interviewee. How about providing opportunity for further education, I'd love to know?

Knox: It depends on our requirement of work.

Hujie: I think so.

Knox: OK. So much for today, let's conclude our talk, shall we?

Hujie: All right. I'm sure that I could do the work well. I also feel that I have the necessary qualifications. I've enjoyed meeting and talking with you.

Knox: Frankly, I'm very favorably impressed by you. Since talking with you, I feel even more strongly that you are perhaps the right man for the job.

Hujie: Is it so? Im glad to hear these.

Knox: Naturally we have have to interview other applicants before we make any final decision. Thank you for comimg.

Hujie: Thank you. I appreciate the time you've given me. I'm looking forward to hearing from you soon.

Knox: Sure.

诺克斯：能。比如：我们每年发两次奖金，放三周假，工作时间从上午九点开始到下午五点结束，一周工作五天。

胡　洁：明白啦。你不介意的话，请告诉我多长时间就能重新审定我的薪水？

诺克斯：通常是六个月后。关于工作，你还有什么问题要问吗？

胡　洁：是的。我还想知道是否享有退休制度、养老金制度和医疗保险？

诺克斯：这自然有。我们是国企，应依国家法令办事。

胡　洁：我认为这一点对于应聘者也是至关重要的。我还想知道公司提供再教育的机会吗？

诺克斯：这要根据工作的需要来定。

胡　洁：我认为是这个理。

诺克斯：好吧，今天就谈到这，咱们结束这次谈话好吗？

胡　洁：好的。但我相信我能胜任这项工作，同时我认为我已具备必要的条件。我也很高兴结识你们并与你们交谈。

诺克斯：坦率地说，你给我的印象很好。和你交谈过后，更感到你也许是这项工作最合适的人选。

胡　洁：是吗？我很高兴听到这些。

诺克斯：当然了，我们还要和其余的人交谈，然后才能作出最后的决定。谢谢你的光临。

胡　洁：感谢你为我花费的时间。盼望早而听到你的佳音。

诺克斯：一定。

第一部

Formulaic Communication 日常交际习语

Expressing Consent and Refuse 表达同意与拒绝

1. I would like to accept your invitation. 我愿意接受你的邀请。

2. I have no objection. 我没意见。

3. With pleasure! 十分乐意!

4. You're right! 您说得对!

5. Excellent! 好极啦!

6. Undoubtedly 毫无疑问。

7. I'm sure of that. 我确信这点。

8. I agree to your construction plan. 我同意你们的施工计划。

9. You agree with me, too. 你也同意我。

10. They agree to help our construction. 他们同意帮助我们建设。

1. No, I'm sorry I can't. 不,很遗憾,我不能。

2. I'm very sorry but I must refuse. 很抱歉,我不得不拒绝。

3. I'm sorry, I'm busy tonight. 对不起,今晚我有事。

4. Unfortunately, I have a prior engagement. 很可惜,我已有约会了。

5. You're wrong. 你说的不对。

6. I'm afraid that I can't agree with you. 恐怕我不同意你的意见。

7. It isn't allowed. 这是不允许的。

8. That's impossible. 这是不可能的。

9. That won't do. 那办不到;不行。

10. No, I don't think so. 不,我认为不是这样的。

Explanatory Notes注释：

英语告别用语（English Parting Expressions）也很多，为了使用方便起见，这里列举部分较常见的告别用语以便在不同场合选择使用：

1. Good night! 晚安，回答 Good night! 晚安。是晚间分别时用语，估计这天不会再见面的客套用语。

2. Good-bye! 再见，回答 Good-bye! 再见。是分手时最常用的一句话，较正式用语。也可以写成 Good-by! （美语）在口语中常用 Bye 或 Bye-bye! 则为较随便的告别用语。Bye-bye! 和 See you later/again. 相比，语气更轻快、更随便。也是美国人的常用语。

3. So long. （美语）再见，回答 So long. 再见。用于彼此十分熟悉的人之间，是很随便的告别用语。在正式场合，以不用为宜。

4. See you later/again. 回头/过会见，回答 See you later/again. 再见/过会见。常用在平时暂别，没有约定下次再见面的时间。而在日常会话中却说 See you. 以简略的形式表达 See you later/again. 的意思，前者语气更随便、更轻快、更亲切。

5. I'll be seeing you. 再见，是美国人喜欢的告别用语。

6. Happy landing. 祝您平安，也是送行者向上飞机的人说的告别语。

7. Bon voyage. 是句法语，意思是"一路平安"。

Spoken Practice 口语练习

1. Pair Work:

A acts as an interviewer. B acts as an interviewee who wants to know what kind of engineering and technical personnel A's company requires and what qualifications A enquires.

2. Tell "true" or "false" in accordance with Learn to Speak English:

1) (　　) The interviewer would like to enquire about the qualifications.

2) (　　) The interviewee wants to take up as career as a builder.

3) (　　) I was graduated from a Construction Technical College and my major is Civil and Industrial Architecture.

4) (　　) About the pension scheme, a retirement plan and medical insurance, we do everything according to the regulations of our state.

5) (　　) We pay the salary according to the post. That is to say, the post decides payment.

3. Read & Interpret the Following Passage:

Application for a Position

P. O. Box. No. 1696

Shanghai China

May 18, 2008

P. O. Box. No. 6959

Richard Building Company

New York, N. Y. 1000197

U. S. A.

Dear Sir,

  In answering to your ad. in today's Daily for **Building Engineering and Technical Personnel**, I beg to offer myself as a candidate for the post. My qualifications are as follows:

Place of birth: Shanghai, China

Salary wanted: $ 1000/month.

Age：twenty-two

Education：Graduated from Architectural Engineering Institute

Reason for the post：My major is civil & industrial Architecture. Applying for this post, I study the major in order to apply it and I feel there is further opportunity in my future studying.

If these meet your requirements, please grant me an interview.

Thank you in advance of your early reply.

Yours obediently

Hua Liu

4. **Learn the Following Words by Heart and Pay Attention to short Clipping Words（截短词）或 shortening Words（缩短词）：**

截头词

bicycle = cycle   telephone = phone   omnibus = bus

earthquake = quake   aeroplane = plane   loudspeaker = speaker

去尾词

taxi = taxicab   exam = examination   lab = laboratory

math = mathematics   photo = photograph   min = minimum

max = maximum   ad = advertisement   zoo = zoological gardens

gas = gasoline/gasolene auto = automobile   dorm = dormitory

5. **Marks the Falling or Rising Tone（升调↗或降调↘）and then Read the Following with Correct Intonation：**

1）I'm sorry I must be off.　　　　　（陈述句）

2）Why didn't you tell me the truth?　（特殊疑问句）

3）Let's go to the building site together.（祈使句）

4）How fast they do!　　　　　　　　（感叹句）

5）Can you speak English or Chinese?　（选择疑问句）

6）You're a constructor, aren't you?　（肯定为主的反义疑问句）

7）Give me a hand.　　　　　　　　　（语气委婉的祈使句）

8）I'm so sorry.　　　　　　　　　　（抱歉的肯定句）

9）If you like.　　　　　　　　　　　（疑惑的陈述句）

10）No, this isn't a tool.　　　　　　（不耐烦的陈述句）

6. Substitute the Following Words & Expressions：

Use the following **Architectural Institute & School（建筑院校）** to re place the black words in the following sentence：

Knox：OK. Hujie. I'd like to enquire about your qualification. Which **architectural university** were you graduated from?

诺克斯：好吧，胡杰。我想先询问你的资格。你毕业于哪所**建筑大学**？

Architectural Institute & School ［ˌɑːkiˈtektʃərəl ˈinstitjuːt ənd skuːl］ 建筑院校

Architectural Engineering Institute ［ˌɑːkiˈtektʃərəl ˌendʒiˈniəriŋ ˈinstitjuːt］
建筑工程学院

Civil Engineering Institute ［ˈsivl ˌendʒiˈniəriŋ ˈinstitjuːt］
土木工程学院

Construction Engineering Vocational College ［kənˈstrʌkʃən ˌendʒiˈniəriŋ vouˈkeiʃənˈkɔlidʒ fə staːf］ 建筑工程职业学院

Construction College for Staff ［kənˈstrʌkʃən ˈkɔlidʒ fə staːf］
建筑职工大学

Construction Vocational College ［kənˈstrʌkʃən vouˈkeiʃənl ˈkɔlidʒ］
建筑职业学院

Architectural Engineering School ［ˌɑːkiˈtektʃərəl ˌendʒiˈniəriŋ skuːl］
建筑工程学校

Construction School for Cadres ［kənˈstrʌkʃən skuːl fə ˈkaːdəz］
建筑干部学校

Construction Technical College ［kənˈstrʌkʃən ˈteknikəl ˈkɔlidʒ］
建设技术学院

Building Installers' School ［ˈbildiŋ inˈstɔːləz skuːl］
建筑安装技工学校

Urban & Rural Construction School
［ˈɔːbən ənd ˈruərəl kənˈstrʌkʃən skuːl］ 城乡建设学校

Construction Secondary School for Staff
［kənˈstrʌkʃən ˈsekəndəri skuːl fə staːf］ 建筑职工中专

Architectural University of Science & Technology

［ˌɑːkiˈtektʃərəl ˌjuːniˈvəːsiti əvˈsaiəns ənd tekˈnɔlədʒi］

建筑科技大学

Architectural Scientific Research Institute

［ˌɑːkiˈtektʃərəl ˌsaiənˈtifik riˈsəːtʃ ˈinstitjuːt］建筑科学研究院

Comprehensive University ［ˌkɔmpriˈhensiv ˌjuːniˈvəːsiti］综合大学

University of Liberal Arts ［ˌjuːniˈvəːsiti əv ˈlibərəl ɑːts］文科大学

University of Science & Engineering

［ˌjuːniˈvəːsiti əvˈsaiəns ənd ˌendʒiˈniəriŋ］理工大学

University of Science & Technology

［ˌjuːniˈvəːsiti əvˈsaiəns ənd tekˈnɔlədʒi］科技大学

Situational Dialogic Unit 7

第七情景对话单元

Learn to Speak English

Talking about Jobs

Smith : Hello! Young man, you work on this worksite, don't you?

Zhuge : Yes, sir. As I was graduated from a Construction Technical College, and my major is building installation.

Smith : If you don't mind, please tell me what your job is, management work or technical work?

Zhuge : Certainly not. I'm an electrician and in charge of electrical install-lation on the site.

Smith : Oh, an electrician, pretty good. Your job is able to develop your ability to the full here. because your job concerns using electrical safety of innumberable households or families.

Zhuge : Yes. Responsibility is weighter than Mount Tai.

Smith : You can rest assured. Who is the girl over there, I'd like to know?

Zhuge : She's a welder in our company and also a technician.

Smith : I see. Her skill must be great, right?

Zhuge : Yes, that's unquestionable. She is a top – notch welder and nobody can compare with her.

Smith : That group of boys and girls is your workmates, right?

Zhuge : Yeah. They're engaged installers just now. There're pipers、fitters、riveters、ventilators and others。

Smith : So many. Who's the eld man in front of them?

Zhuge : He is our site director, Mr. Oyang.

Smith : What is he doing over there?

Zhuge : He's giving them a safety lecture. Need I introduce him to you, sir?

Smith : Naturally, you must.

Oyang : How do you do, sir?

Smith : How do you do, director!

Oyang : Please tell me which aspect you like to know, sir?

学说英语

谈论职业

史密斯：喂！年轻人，你在这家建筑工地工作，不是吗？

诸　葛：是的，先生。因为我毕业于一所建设技术学院，学的是建筑安装专业。

史密斯：如果您不介意，请问您是做什么工作的，是从事管理工作还是技术工作？

诸　葛：当然不介意。我是一名电工，负责这家工地的电气安装工作。

史密斯：啊！一名电工，不错，你的工作在建筑工地可大有作为。因为它关系到千家万户今后的用电安全。

诸　葛：是呀，责任重于泰山。

史密斯：没错儿。我想知道那边那位女工是谁？

诸　葛：她是我们公司的一名焊工，技师。

史密斯：我知道啦，她的技术一定很棒，是吧？

诸　葛：是的，这是无可置疑的。她在公司是一流的焊工，无人可此。

史密斯：那一帮男男女女也是你们的工友，对吗？

诸　葛：是啊！他们都是刚应聘来的安装工，有管道工、安装钳工、通风工、铆工等工种。

史密斯：还不少呢。站在他们前面那位长者是谁？

诸　葛：他是我们的工地主任，欧阳先生。

史密斯：他在那里干什么？

诸　葛：他在给他们上安全课。需要我把他介绍给您吗，先生？

史密斯：那是自然的，你必须。

欧　阳：您好，先生？

史密斯：您好，主任！

欧　阳：请问先生想了解哪方面的情况？

Smith: Recruit and use wokers. As it's a super worksite, and construction is intense but keeps in regular order, news of victory keeps poring in. so I'm very interested in your recruit and use wokers here. Can you tell me how many constructors there are on your site?

Oyang: OK. Over thousand. Almost 10% is engineering & technical and managerial personnel.

Smith: Technical & managerial personnel and workers proportion is reasonable. Which kinds of tradesmen are there now?

Oyang: There're bricklayers, carpenters and plasterers. The main structures are going to be finished. So some civil construction workers are leaving here and installers and decorators are coming soon.

Smith: I see. Maybe you have enough skilled workers to accomplish your production task. But why don't you consider to train some local people?

Oyang: Yes. Good idea. We'll employ several hundred local people during the construction peak period.

Smith: Good. Employing local people take part in your construction, in this way, it can not only solve thire problem of geting a job but also pick up your speed of construction .

Oyang: It really satisfies both sides.

Smith: It's a fine thing, but how do you make sure that construction quality won't be affection.

Oyang: According to construction stage, we should class and train some local employees to get working skills as early as possible and promote their consciousness about quality and safety.

Smith: Yes, they'll improve your working efficiency a lot and guaranteen construction tasks accomplish on schedule.

Oyang: Oh. I see, sir. Thank you very much for your advice.

Smith: Not at all.

史密斯：用工。这是一个超大工地，而且施工紧张有序，捷报频传，所以我对你们工地的用工很感兴趣。您能告诉我这儿有多少建筑施工人员吗？

欧　阳：好的。有 1000 多人，其中约 10% 是工程技术和管理人员。

史密斯：技术和管理人员以及工人的比例很合理。现有哪些工种？

欧　阳：有瓦工、木工和粉刷工。由于主体工程即将结束，一些土建工人即将离开此地，而安装工和装饰工很快就要进驻工地。

史密斯：我知道啦！也许你们有足够的技术工人来完成你们的生产任务。不过你们怎么也没考虑培训一些当地人吧？

欧　阳：考虑过，好主意。我们在施工高峰期间将要招聘几百名当地人。

史密斯：好。雇用当地人参与施工不仅解决了他们就业问题而且加快了你们的施工进度。

欧　阳：这是件两全其美的好事。

史密斯：是件好事，但怎样保证施工质量不受影响呢？

欧　阳：根据施工的不同阶段，我们会尽快分类地培训他们的工作技能，以提高质量和安全意识。

史密斯：对呀！当地工人会极大地帮助你们提高工作效率，确保你们的施工如期完成。

欧　阳：啊，我明白！非常感谢你的指点，先生。

史密斯：没什么。

Formulaic Communication 日常交际习语

Asking Job and Responses 询问职业与应答

1. What's your job? 你做什么工作？

    ——I'm a Chinese builder. 我是一名中国建筑工人。

2. What do you do? 你干什么工作？

    ——I'm a student and learn building engineering cost.

    我是一名大学生，学建筑工程造价。

3. What's your occupation? 你的职业是什么？

    ——I'm a civil engineer. 我是一名土木工程师。

4. What sort of work do you do? 你干哪种工作？

    ——I'm an inspector on a construction site.

    我是一位在一家建筑工地工作的工程监理。

5. Where do you work? 你在哪儿工作？

    ——I work in Xi'an. 我在西安工作。

6. Are you on day shift or night shift? 你是上白班还是上夜班？

    ——Sometimes day shift, sometimes night shift. 有时上白班，有时上夜班。

第一部

Explanatory Notes注释：

1. job 既可指固定工作也可指临时性的工作，用于可数名词时，有单复数形式。job 的相对意思是 out of work "失业"。例如：He has a job. 他得到一份工作。College graduate wants to a job, any sort of job is OK. 大学毕业生想找份工作，任何工作都行。

2. work 的意思也是"工作"，只能用于不可数名词，所以没有单复数形式。work 这里的工作指的是固定工作，常用来与 rest "休息"相对。例如：He is at work. 他正在工作（做事）。Unskill young people cannot find work in the city. 无技能的年轻人在城里不好找到工作。Works 并非是 work 的复数形式而是有其他意思，表示著作、工程、工厂等。例如：a cement works 水泥厂，public works 公共事业，works by Lu Xun 鲁迅的著作。

3. 英语中 pardon 和 forgive "对不起"的表达场合：

   1）pardon 是口头用语，表示原谅，饶恕之意，在没有听清对方的话，请再说一遍时的"对不起"，用升调。例如：
   I beg your pardon ↗. = Would you mind say it again? 对不起，请再说一遍。
   I beg your pardon ↗. 可以说 Beg your pardon ↗. 也可以说 Pardon ↗均表达了相同之意。

   2）forgive 是书面用语，原谅，饶恕，宽恕之意，一般用在对方有情绪却难以平息时。例如：
   Please forgive me for being rude. 请原谅我的鲁莽。
   You're forgiven. 你得到了宽恕。

Spoken Practice 口语练习

1. Pair Work：

Imagine that you have been invited to a party. Discuss with your partner how to give your introduction each other (including your major, job, company, worksite, etc).

2. Answer the Following Questions in accordance with Learn to Speak English：

1) Which school was Zhuge graduated from?

2) Is she a new electrician or veteran welder?

3) Which tradesmen always do the work of the main structure?

4) What types of work in production must come to the site when the main structure is OK?

5) You should employ the local people to help you work, shouldn't you? Why?

3. Read & Interpret the Following Passage：

Types of Work in Construction Production

There are four main types of work in building production. They are civil construction workers, building installers, building mechanics and building decorators. Of course, each of these includes more than eight types. For example, building installers can be divided into plumber, electrician, welder, hoister, ventilating worker, riveter, fitter and so on. Among tradesmen set in closing coordination, not a single one of them can be dispensed with. Each tradesman plays an important part in construction.

4. Giev the Following Compounds Chinese Meaning, and Learn the Following Words by Heart：

$$n. + n. = n.$$

1) classroom	Englishman	note-book
2) worksite	mortherland	time-table
3) guesthouse	grandfather	trolley-bus

4）earthwork　　　　greenhouse　　　　water-pipe

5）framework　　　　concretemixer　　　water-tower

5. Read the Following Sentences. Pay Attention to Assimilations（音的同化）：

1）I'm glad to meet you.［aim glæd tə miːtʃu］

2）Did you see him?［di dʒu siːhim］

3）Does she like it? Of course she does.　［dʌʃ ʃi laik it? əv kɔʒ ʃi dʌz］

4）I haven't seen him these years.［ai 'havnt siːn him ðiːʒ ʒəːz］

5）We used to practise on the construction site.［wi juːst tə præktis ɔn ðə kən'strʌkʃ ən sait］

6. Substitute the Following Words & Expressions：

Use the following **Construction Tradesmen**（建筑施工工种）to replace the black words in the following sentence：

Smith：If you don't mind, please tell me what your **job** is, management work or technical work?

史密斯：如果您不介意，请问您是干什么工作的？是从事管理工作还是技术工作？

Zhuge：Certainly not. I'm an **electrician** and in charge of electrical installlation on the site.

诸　葛：肯定不介意。我是一名**电工**，负责这家工地的电气安装工作。

Construction Tradesmen［kən'strʌkʃən 'treidzmen］建筑施工工种

civil construction worker［'sivl kən'strʌkʃən 'wəːkə］土（木）建（筑）工人

bricklayer［'brik₁leiə］瓦工

road builder［roud 'bildə］筑路工

carpenter［'kaːpintə］（粗）木工，木匠

steel fixer/bender［stiːl 'fiksə 'bendə］钢筋工

concrete worker［'kɔnkriːt 'wəːkə］混凝土工

stone mason［stoun 'meisn］石工

scaffolder ［'skæfəldə］架子工

building installer ［'bildiŋ in'ɔtə.lə］建筑安装工人

plumber ［'plʌmə］水暖工，管工

electrician ［ilek'triʃən］电工

fitter ［'fitə］安装钳工

welder ［'weldə］焊工

riveter ［'rivitə］铆工

ventilator ［'ventileitə］通风工

building mechanic ［'bildiŋ mi'kænik］建筑机械工人

turner ［'tə:nə］车工

assembler ［ə'semblə］装配工

machine repairman ［mə'ʃi:n ri'pɛərmən］机修工

driver ［'draivə］司机

hoister ［'hɔistə］起重机司机

crane operator ［krein 'ɔpəreitə］吊车司机

bulldozer operator ［'bul,douzə 'ɔpəreitə］推土机手

scraper operator ［'skeipə 'ɔpəreitə］铲土机手

excavator operator ［'ekskəveitə 'ɔpəreitə］挖土机手

loader operator ［'loudə 'ɔpəreitə］装载机手

pneumatic drill operator ［nju(:)'mætik drill 'ɔpəreitə］风钻工

air-compressor operator ［ɛə kəm'presə 'ɔpəreitə］空压机工

building decorator ［'bildiŋ 'dekəreitə］建筑装饰工人

joiner ［'dʒɔinə］细木工

plasterer ［'pla:stərə］粉刷工、粉灰工

painter ［'peintə］油漆工

glazier ［'gleizjə］玻璃安装工

asphalt/ asphaltum layer ［æs'fælt æs'fæltəm 'leiə］油毡工

other tradesmen ［'ʌðə 'treidzmen］其他工种

tester ［'testə］实验工

warehouse keeper ［'wɛəhaus 'ki:pə］料工，料工/库管员

surveyor ［sə(:)'veiə］测量工

blacksmith ［ˈblæksmiθ］ 锻工，铁匠

contract worker ［ˈkɔntrækt ˈworker］ 合同工

assistant ［əˈsistənt］ 小工，助手

apprentice ［əˈprentis］ 学徒工，初学者

master ［ˈmɑːstə］ 师傅

young worker ［yʌŋ ˈwəːkə］ 青（年）工（人）

veteran ［ˈvetərən］ 老手，富有经验的工人

skilled worker ［skild ˈwəːkə］ 熟练工人

veteran worker ［ˈvetərən ˈwəːkə］ 老工人

technician ［tekˈniʃən］ 技师

Situational Dialogic Unit **8**

第八情景对话单元

Learn to Speak English

Talking about Characteristics of Windows

Gaoji: Why is computer "Windows" very popular with people nowadays, professor Wood?

Wood: Because its designing has been improved too much, function is more and operation is quite easy.

Gaoji: Excuse me, I don't know what GUI is?

Wood: GUI is the abbreviation for graphical user interface.

Gaoji: I see. What is the computer screen referred to in windows?

Wood: It is referred to as a desktop.

Gaoji: And what is usage of it?

Wood: It displays all your work in rectangular areas called windows.

Gaoji: Right. But how to operate it?

Wood: You open a window when you run an application and close the window when you quit from an application program.

Gaoji: That's quite good. What do you easily drag a window to change its size and location with?

Wood: With the mouse. You arrange windows on the desktop just as you move work items around on your actual desk.

Gaoji: And what does multitask operation mean in Windows?

Wood: With Windows, you will find it easy to start up and work with application programs.

Gaoji: How does it apply easily?

Wood: You can run more the one application at a time, transfer information between them and switch quickly among them.

Gaoji: Wonderful! This is why windows are popularized and widely used.

Wood: Yes, It's true.

学说英语

谈论 Windows 的特性

高　技：为什么当今计算机 Windows 颇受人们的宠爱，伍德教授？

伍　德：由于设计改善了许多，功能多，而且操作简便。

高　技：抱歉，我不懂得什么是 GUI？

伍　德：GUI 是图形用户界面的缩写。

高　技：我清楚了。在 windows 中，计算机的屏幕叫什么？

伍　德：计算机的屏幕叫桌面。

高　技：那桌面有什么用处？

伍　德：在桌面上，你所有的工作都显示在一个叫窗口的矩形区域里。

高　技：对，但怎样进行操作呢？

伍　德：你运行一个应用程序时，就打开一个窗口，从应用程序中退出时，就关闭相应窗口。

高　技：相当不错。你用什么方法很容易拖动窗口以改变窗口的大小和位置？

伍　德：使用鼠标。在桌面上排列窗口，就像你在实际的桌面上移动工作用品一样容易。

高　技：那么，什么是 Windows 的任务操作呢？

伍　德：在 Windows 中，你会发现启动、运行应用程序都很简单。

高　技：怎样简便地使用？

伍　德：在某一时刻可以同时运用多个应用程序，在它们之间传递信息以及它们之间快速地切换。

高　技：太好啦！这就是 Windows 为什么得到普及和广泛应用的原因。

伍　德：是的，的确是这样。

Formulaic Communication 日常交际习语

Expressing Apologies, Regrets and Responses 表达道歉，遗憾与应答

1. Excuse me. 对不起。

　　——Certainly. 请。

2. Oh, pardon me. 请原谅。

　　——It quite all right. 没关系。

3. (I'm awfully) sorry. （我很）抱歉。

　　——That's doesn't matter. 没关系。

4. Please forgive me for interrupting you. 请原谅我打断你的话。

　　——It really isn't worth mentioning. You're forgiven. 那真是件不值得
　　　一提的事。你得到宽恕了。

5. I'm sorry to have/that I have kept you waiting for a long time.
　　对不起，让你久等了。

　　——I accept your apology. Let's just laugh it off. 我接受你的道歉，咱
　　　们就一笑了之吧。

6. Don't be angry! That isn't your fault. 别生气！那不是你的错。

7. Unfortunatly, I have no more time. 真遗憾，我没时间。

8. What a pity/shame! 真可惜/遗憾！

9. It was most thoughtless of me. I must apologize to you.
　　我太鲁莽了，我得向你道歉。

10. Don't think any more about it. We all quite understand you.
　　可别再去想它了，我们都完全理解你的用心。

Explanatory Notes注释：

1. **中国人名和地名的拼法**（**Spelling Chinese Names of people and Places**）是按照国务院颁发的普通话拼写方案实施——汉语拼音字母拼写。其读音以汉语为基础，而将汉语的四声换成英语的轻重声。若有两个音节两个都重读，若有三个音节可三个都重读，中间音节也可不重读。

1）汉语姓名分姓氏和名字两部分，姓氏和名字要分开写而且第一个字母都必须大写。如：杨利华——Yang Lihua。对于笔名和化名也按真名拼写。如：鲁迅——Lu Xun。对于原有惯用拉丁字母拼写的名人的姓名也用该方案，有必要时可附注在括号或注释中。如：毛泽东——Mao Zedong（Mao Tse-tung），对于汉语的名也可缩写。如：杨利华——Yang Lihua 或 Yang L. H，为了符合国际名字在姓氏前的写法，也可拼写为 Lihua Yang 或 L. H Yang。

2）中国地名也用汉语拼音拼写，第一个字母也应大写，整个地名连写无须加连字符号，沿用已久的英译地名可注在括号内。如：黄河——Huanghe（Yellow River）、北京——Beijing（Peking）、广东——Guangdong（Canton）. 但地名用作形容词时，所修饰的普通名词，则以小写起头。如：中国茶——chinese tea。

2. 英语中 **excuse me** 和 **sorry** 都是表示歉意的词，虽然这两个词的汉语意思均可译为"对不起"，但在用法上却不尽相同，容易造成混淆，所以至少得掌握两点。一是从时间概念上讲，在事发之前，因说话人要打扰别人，以表示礼貌，应使用 **excuse me**。比如要从拥挤的人群通过或打断别人们谈话时，通常要说 Exuse me. 对不起。对方回答 Certainly. 请吧/可以。在事发后，因过失、失礼或冒犯他人，比如踩了别人的脚或冲撞了他人时，应立即向对方表示歉意，说声 Sorry. 对不起。对方也就会说 It's nothing. 没什么。二是从句型结构上讲，**excuse me ＋ for doing sth. 或 excuse one's doing sth. 句型**。例如："对不起，打扰你一下。"应译为 Excuse me for interrupting you. 或 Excuse my interrupting you. 如用 Sorry 时，其句型则是 **Sorry ＋ to do sth. 或 Sorry ＋ that C**。例如："对不起，我没听懂你的话。"应译为 I'm sorry that I didn't catch what you said. 或 I'm sorry not to catch what you said.

Spoken Practice 口语练习

1. Pair Work：

Imagine that you have some computering knowledge, maybe "Windows" is very popular with your classmates, but you want to improve your operating skill and you are discussing how to grasp the operative ability as quick as possible.

2. Tell "true" or "false" in accordance with Learn to Speak English：

1) (　　) Computers' designing "Windows" has been improved, so function is more and operation is quite easy.

2) (　　) The computer screen is referred to change its size and location with mouse in windows.

3) (　　) With the mouse, you easily drag a window.

4) (　　) The meaning of GUI is a graphical user interface.

5) (　　) More than two programs can be run at the same time in windows

3. Read & Interpret the Following Passage：

Office Automation

Today's organizations have a wide variety of office automation hardware and software components. These components are intended to automate a task or function that is presently performed manually. But experts agree that the key to attaining office automation lies in integration—incorporating all the components into a whole system so that this goal can be accomplished when computer, communication and office equipments are networked and an office worker can be easily access the entire system through a personal computer sitting in his/her desk.

4. Read and Learn the following Useful Synonyms（同义）by Heart：

synonym	meaning	synonym	synonym	meaning	synonym
above	在上	over	each	每一	every
accept	接受	receive	fast	快	quick
add	加上	plus	get	取	take
ago	以前	before	glad	快乐	happy
all	全部	whole	good	好	fine

续表

synonym	meaning	synonym	synonym	meaning	synonym
also	也是	too	hear	听	listen
always	经常	often	high	高	tall
back	后面	behind	hope	希望	wish
begin	开始	start	ill	病	sick
big	大	large	learn	学习	study
boat	船	ship	look	看	see
broad	宽阔	wide	people	人	persons
city	城市	town	speak	谈话	talk
close	接近	near	street	街道	road
correct	正确的	right	understand	明白	know
difficult	困难	hard	want	需要	need
dress	衣服	clothes	world	世界	earth

5. Mark Which Word Should Be Stressed according to Stress Rule（重读规则），and then Practise Reading the Following Sentences：

1）We should work hard at English and computer.

2）How old are you，sir?

3）There are many multi-storey buildings in every city nowadays.

4）Are you Chinese Builders? Yes，we are.

5）Tom is typewriting faster because he practises more.

6. Substitute the Following Words & Expressions：

Use the following **Computers' Hardware and Others**（计算机硬件和其他）to replace the black words in the following sentence：

Wood：With **the mouse.** You arrange **windows** on **the desktop** just as you move work items around on your actual desk.

伍　德：使用**鼠标**。在**桌面**上排列**窗口**，就像你在实际的桌面上移动工作用品一样容易。

Computers' Hardware and Others［kəm'pju：təz'ha：dwɛə ənd 'ʌðəz］计算机硬件和其他

hard/fixed disk［ha：d fiksd disk］硬盘

cathode-ray tube（CRT）［ˈkæθoud rei tjuːb］显示器

mainframe［ˈmeinfreim］主机

mouse［maus］鼠标

chip［tʃip］芯片

data bus［ˈdeitə bʌs］数据总线

tracks［træks］磁道

memory［ˈmeməri］内存储器，内存

serial port［ˈsiəriəl pɔːt］串行接口

parallel port［ˈpærəlel pɔːt］并行接口

heads［hedz］磁头

screen［griːn］屏幕

drive［ˈdraiv］驱动器

printer［ˈprintə］打印机

scanner［ˈskænə］扫描仪/器

display［disˈplei］显示器

monitor［ˈmɔnitə］监视器

diskette［ˈdiskit］软盘

master［ˈmaːstə］［计］主盘

slave［sleiv］［计］从盘

keyboard［ˈkiːˌbɔːd］键盘

Space［speis］空格键

Enter［ˈentə］回车

Backspace［ˈbækspeis］回格

Delete［diˈliːt］删除

Insert［inˈsəːt］插入

Shift［ˈʃift］上档

Cap Lock［kæp lɔk］大写锁定

central processing unit（CPU）

［ˈsentrəl ˈprousesiŋ ˈjuːnit］中央处理器

bus interface unit（BIU）［bʌs ˈintəfeis ˈjuːnit］总线接口单元

Situational Dialogic Unit **9**

第九情景对话单元

Learn to Speak English

Talking about Object Oriented Programming

Minjie: I've a question to ask, teacher.

Hunter: OK. What question?

Minjie: What is Object Oriented Programming (OOP)?

Hunter: New way. It's a new way of approaching the job of programming.

Minjie: It differs from traditional programming, right?

Hunter: That's right. It uses objects as data structures to enhance productivity, simplify programming, and improve software reliability.

Minjie: Oh, I see. What characteristics does OOP have?

Hunter: All Object Oriented Programming languages have three characteristics in common: object, polymorphism and inheritance.

Minjie: Sorry I'm still not quite sure what the object is, please explain it to me?

Hunter: OK. Object is a data structure that contains both structured information and related operations.

Minjie: Great! Can an object contain other objects?

Hunter: Yes. In this way, the object is given both data properties and behaviors.

Minjie: I see. Can object oriented programs better reflect the real world they're trying to simulate?

Hunter: Right. You're so clever.

Minjie: I got it. Thanks a lot, teacher.

Hunter: Don't mention it.

学说英语

谈论面向对象的程序设计

敏　杰：老师，我有个问题要请教。

亨　特：说吧，什么问题？

敏　杰：什么是面向对象的程序设计？

亨　特：新方法。它是一种新的编程方法。

敏　杰：新编程法与传统的编程方法有所不同，对吗？

亨　特：对。它把使用对象作为其数据结构以提高效率，简化程序，提高软件可靠性。

敏　杰：哦，我明白了。面向对象的程序设计有哪些特点呢？

亨　特：所有的面向对象的程序设计语言都具有三个共同的特性：对象、多态和继承。

敏　杰：对不起，我不懂什么叫对象，请给我解释一下行吗？

亨　特：行。对象是一种数据结构，它既包含有结构的信息又包含有相关的操作。

敏　杰：棒极了！一个对象能够涵盖另一些对象吗？

亨　特：是的。通过这种方式，对象就赋予数据特征和行为。

敏　杰：我明白啦！使用面向对象的程序设计能更好地反应程序欲模拟的现实世界吗？

亨　特：对。你真聪明。

敏　杰：我懂了。多谢，老师。

亨　特：甭客气。

Formulaic Communication 日常交际习语

Expressing Good Wishes 表达祝愿

1. (I wish you) good luck. 祝您好运气!

2. Pleasant journey (to you)! 祝您旅途愉快!

3. Have a good/nice time. 祝您玩得高兴/痛快。

4. All the best! 万事无意!

5. Keep well! 祝您健康长寿!

6. Don't forget us! 别忘了我们!

7. Give everyone my best regards. 请代我向大家问好。

8. Please remember me to your parents. 请替我向你父母问好。

9. I hope everything goes well with you. 希望你一帆风顺。

10. Hope you enjoy your visit to someplace. 祝你某地之行快乐。

1. Thank you. 谢谢。

2. The same to you. 也祝贺你。

3. Thank you, you too. 谢谢你, 你也一样。

Explanatory Notes注释：

1. 外国人互相问好和再见时常用 Morning! 代替 Good morning! 用 See you. 代替 See you later/again. 这种说法对于初学英语或接触外国人较少者可能觉得有点怪或不完全明白其意。实际上这种说法是英语口语的简化表达方式。语言是人们思想情感交流的工具，随着社会的发展，生活节奏的加快，人们就会使用更简短的语言传递信息，以达到交流思想的目的。也许有些人从未听过，也未见过，也根本不清楚 Gonna work? Wanna help? Ya gotta got? 的意思，但这些人就未必是初学者，而是因为 Gonna, Wanna, Ya gotta 这些词是美国口语中常用的词，也可能还未收录到英语词典中。如果这样写 Are you going to work ＝ Gonna work?（你上班去?）Do you want to help (me)? ＝ Wanna help?（你想帮我吗?）Do you have got to go ＝ Ya gotta got?（你一定要走吗?）就会一目了然。这些实例说明了英语简化表达的重要性。

2. 在一个单词后加了后缀，就改变了单词词性（即加后缀变词性）。

3. 在回答对方问话时，要表示含义不十分明确，比较含糊，不十分确定的答语时，常用 perhaps（也许），I think /hope /believe/suppose / expect so.（我想/希望/相信/料想是这样），It's quite probable.（完全有可能。）等。

Spoken Practice口语练习

1. Pair Work：

Work in group or pairs. Supposing A is as a student. B is as a teacher who teaches computer application. After the class of object oriented programming, A still has some questions to ask. A and B talk about them.

2. Tell "true" or "false" in accordance with Learn to Speak English：

1) (   ) Object Oriented Programming is the name of a piece of software.

2) (   ) An object can not contain other objects.

3) (   ) Using OOP can simplify the process of writing programs.

4) (   ) OOP is a new software of programming and more productive than traditional programming.

5) (   ) All Object Oriented Programming languages usually have some characteristics：object, polymorphism and inheritance.

3. Read & Interpret the Following Passage：

AutoCAD Basics

AutoCAD is popular CAD program because it can be customized to suit and an individual's needs. On the AutoCAD screen, there are：

1. Title bar—this will show you what program you are running and what the current filename is. 2. Pull-down menus—these are the standard pull-down menus through which you can access all commands. 3. Main toolbar—this has most of the standard Windows icons as well as the most common AutoCAD commands. 4. Drawing space—this is where you have almost infinite area to draw. 5. Status Bar—this allows to see and change different modes of drawing.

4. Add to Some words or Phraises If necessery and then gave Chinese meaning：

(Cuel Words——B meets his frend A on the way when B is going to town and buy something. They both have a dialogue.)

A．Where to? _____?

B：Down town. _____．

A：What for? _____?

B：Shopping. _____．

A：In a hurry? _____?

B：Rather. _____．

5. Learn the Following Pronounces by Heart and Pay Attention to the Changing Forms：

1）nowhere   nobody   nothing   no one

2）anywhere   any body   anything   anyone

3）everywhere   everybody   everything   everyone

4）somewhere   somebody   something   someone

5）whatever   whenever   whoever   wherever

6. Substitute the Following Words & Expressions：

Use the following **Computers' Software and others**（计算机软件以及其他）to replace the black words in the following sentence：

Hunter：New way. It's a new way of approaching the job of **programming.**

亨　特：新方法。它是一种新的**编程**方法。

Computers' Software and others ［kəm'pju：təz'sɔftwεə ənd 'ʌðəz］
计算机软件以及其他

Winner ［'winə］万能财务软件

wordstar（W. S.）［wə：d'sta：］字处理软件

multi-user system ［'mʌlti 'juzə 'sistəm］多用户系统

disk operating system（DOS）［disk 'ɔpəreitiŋ 'sistim］操作系统

program（me）［'prougræm］程序

edit ［'edit］编辑

data ［'deitə］数据

backcup ［bæk'kʌp］备份

format ［'fɔ：mæt］格式化（磁盘）

copy ［'kɔpi］拷贝，复制

character ［'kæriktə］字符

fonts ［fɔnts］字体

megabyte（MB）［'megə‚bait］兆字节

gigabyte（GB）［'dʒigə‚bait］千兆字节

kilobyte（KB）［'ki：lou‚bait］千字节

electronic mail（E-mail）［ilek'trɔnik meil］电子邮件

network ［'netwə：k］计算机网络

multimedia ［‚mʌlti'medjə］多媒体

configuration ［kən‚figju'reiʃən］配置，构造

Internet ［'intənet］（国际）互联网

visual（s）［'vizjuəl（s）］画面，可视资料

computer virus ［kəm'pju：tə 'vaiərəs］计算机病毒

performance ［pə'fɔ：məns］性能，工作状况

default ［di'fɔ：lt］默认（值）

database ［'deitəbeis］数据库，资料库

capacity ［kə'pæsiti］容量；能力

application ［‚æpli'keiʃən］应用程序

restart ［'ri：'sta：t］重新启动

word processing ［wə：d'prousesiŋ］文字处理

online ［ɔn'lain］联机，在互联网上

auto repeat ［'ɔ：tou ri'pi：t］自动重复

wipe out data ［waip aut 'deitə］消除数据

delete file ［di'li：t fail］删除文件

system halted ［'sistəm 'hɔ：ltid］系统暂停

access denied ［'ækses di'naid］拒绝访问

base/extended/total memory ［beis iks'tendid'toutl'meməri］基本/扩展/总内存

TEST Of PART ONE   第一部   测试题

1. **Choose the Best Answer:**

1) "**How are you**?" should answer _____ Very well, thanks.

   A. How do you do?   B. Fine, thank you. And you?

   C. How are you?   D. I'm OK.

2) An alternative form of **I beg your pardon** is _____.

   A. Excuse me   B. wrong   C. OK.   D. Thak you

3) If you **are about to return home** that means that you _____.

   A. have just returned home

   B. are hesitant about returning home

   C. are just going to return home

   D. are on the point of returning home

4) If you meet a distinguished guest at the first time, you'd better greet him with _____.

   A. How are you?   B. Good morning, sir.

   C. How do you do?   D. Hi

5) When someone concludes the main idea or main point, she shouldn't say _____.

   A. Are you still with me?   B. all in all.

   C. to cut a long story short.

   D. to put the whole thing in a nutshell.

6) If you need a help, you should start _____.

   A. Excuse me   B. Sorry   C. OK.   D. Pardon

7) Which sentence isn't similar to 'What is your job?'? _____.

   A. What sort of work do you do?

   B. What are you doing now?

   C. What's your occupation?

   D. What do you do?

8) When someone terminates his conversation, he shouldn't say _____.

   A. It's very nice to talk with you, but I'm afraid I can't stay any longer...

   B. I'm awfully sorry, but I'm meeting somebody in two minutes.

C. I hope you'll forgive me but I really have to be going. . .

D. I don't know if I make myself clear?

9）Which of the following words is pronounced as two syllables?

A. hoped   B. looked   C. lasted   D. paid

10）**By the way** in spoken English means _____.

A. incidentally   B. in the way

C. on the way   D. by way of

11）A common synonym for **decide** is _____.

A. make use of   B. make from

C. make up one's minde D. make up to

12）Many builders **are used to** reading English in the morning on the worksite when they construct abroad.

A. are accustomed to   B. used to

C. accustom to   D. was used to.

13）Noun of the words '**contract, present, use**' should be _____.

A. ［'kɔntrækt 'present juː z］   B. ［'kɔntrækt pre'sent juː s］

C. ［kən'trækt 'present juː s］   D. ［'kɔntrækt 'present juː s］

14）Which of the following has not any **Loss of Plosion**.

A. at that time   B. looking   C. sit down   D. blackboard

15）Which **intonation marks** of the following sentences is incorrect?

A. Do you have a computer in your ↗ office now? No, I ↘ don't.

B. Do you speak ↗ English or ↗ Chinese?

C. There are so many beautiful houses ↘ around us, aren't ↗ there?

D. Are there any up-to date machines on your ↗ worksite?

Yes, there ↘ are

2. Many Words in English Can Be Used as either Nouns or Verbs：

1）excuse _____ n. _____ v.

2）look _____ n. _____ v.

3）work _____ n. _____ v.

4）study _____ n. _____ v.

5）house _____ n. _____ v.

6) practice _____ n. _____ v.

7) question _____ n. _____ v.

8) use _____ n. _____ v.

9) master _____ n. _____ v.

10) building _____ n. _____ v.

Write sentences to illustrate the use of these words as nouns and as verbs

3. Give Plural of the Following Nouns：

Brush _____   box _____

city _____   zero _____

half _____   foot _____

roof _____   mouse _____

hero _____   shelf _____

deer _____   grown-up

looker-on _____   editor-in-chief _____

4. Make Sentences with the Following phrases：

1) to conform to. . . _____

2) to look forward to. . . _____

3) to depend on. . . _____

4) to catch up with . . . _____

5) not only. . . but also. . . _____

6) to integrate. . . with . . . _____

7) all in all _____

8) to get used to. . . _____

9) to spend. . . in. . . _____

10) in order to . . . _____

5. Complete the following according to Chinese Given：

A：Where to ?　　去哪儿?　　_____

B：Worksite.　　去工地。　　_____

A：What for?　　去干什么?　　_____

B：Working.　　工作。　　_____

A：In a hurry?　　急吗?　　_____

B：Rather.　　很急。

6. Give the International Phonetic Symbols（国际音标）and Chinese Meaning of the Following Words，and pay attention to inform with Spellings rules（不符合读音规则的拼写）：

answer［ˈaːnsə］（回答）（w 不发音） autumn ［   ］（   ）（   ）

build ［   ］（   ）（   ） business ［   ］（   ）（   ）

busy ［   ］（   ）（   ） forehead ［   ］（   ）（   ）

handsome ［   ］（   ）（   ） island ［   ］（   ）（   ）

muscle ［   ］（   ）（   ） paradigm ［   ］（   ）（   ）

plumber ［   ］（   ）（   ） receipt ［   ］（   ）（   ）

southern ［   ］（   ）（   ） Wednesday ［   ］（   ）（   ）

7. Give the International Phonetic Symbols（国际音标）of the Following Words（同形异音异义词），and Pay Attention to Their Pronunciation and Meaning：

bow ［ bau ］n. 船头   bow ［ bou ］n. 弓

conduct ［   ］n. 行为   conduct ［   ］v. 传导

contract ［   ］n. 合同   contract ［   ］v. 承包

lead ［   ］v. 引导   lead ［   ］n. 铅

minute ［   ］n. 分钟   minute ［   ］adj. 详细的

nice ［   ］adj. 好的   Nice ［   ］n. 尼斯（港口）

permit ［   ］n. 许可证   permit ［   ］v. 允许

present ［   ］adj. 出席的   present ［   ］v. 交出

produce ［   ］n. 产品   produce ［   ］v. 生产

project ［   ］n. 计划   project ［   ］v. 设计

read ［   ］v. 读   read ［   ］v. 读（的过去时）

record ［   ］n. 唱片   record ［   ］v. 记录

supply ［   ］v. 供给   supply ［   ］ad. 柔软地

subject ［   ］n. 主语   subject ［   ］v. 使隶属

use ［   ］n. 用法   use ［   ］v. 应用

8. Give a Brief Introdutcion Yourself in English：（You can introduce your school/college、major、subjects、English and computer's level as more as possible.）

Part Two
English Conversations with Constructors' Life abroad
(Situational Dialogic Unit 10 – 20)

第二部
建筑施工人员国外生活英语情景会话
（第十至第二十情景对话单元）

Situational Dialogic Unit 10

第十情景对话单元

Learn to Speak English

Talking about Chinese Constructors at the Customs（Exit & Entry）

Anna：Your passport, please.

Lima：Here it is, miss.

Anna：OK. Keep good custody of it. Show me your documents, please.

Lima：Just a minute, they're in my briefcase. Oh, here's my visa and the health certificate and vaccination papers.

Anna：Let me have a look. How long will you stay here?

Lima：At least two years.

Anna：Which is your baggage, please?

Lima：These two suitcases and this briefcase are all mine.

Anna：I see. Anything to declare?

Lima：Oh, nothing.

Anna：Would you mind opening your suitcase? I'd like to have a look.

Lima：All right, miss, please.

Anna：Your video camera belongs to the valuable article. It isn't duty free. You have to pay the Customs duty according to regulation.

Lima：Sorry, I don't know this. I'm a builder and it's my first time to transit. How much should I pay for it?

Anna：Let me check. Oh, you have to pay ＄100 at least.

Lima：To pay taxes according to regulation is every citizen's bounden duty. OK. Here you are.

Anna：What you said is right. Here is your duty receipt and take care of it, please. The inspection is over. You're through now.

Lima：Thank you.

学说英语

谈论中国建筑施工人员通关（出入境）

安　娜：请出示你的护照。

李　杩：小姐，这是我的护照。

安　娜：好的。保管好。请出示您的其他证件。

李　杩：等一会儿，证件都装在公文包里。啊，这是我的签证，健康证和预防接种证。

安　娜：让我看一看。您在这里逗留多久？

李　杩：至少两年。

安　娜：请问哪一个是你的行李？

李　杩：这两个箱子和这个公文包都是我的。

安　娜：我知道了。有什么东西需要报关吗？

李　杩：哦，没什么。

安　娜：请您把箱子打开好吗？我想看一看。

李　杩：好的，小姐，请看吧！

安　娜：您的摄像机属于贵重物品，不属免税物，你得照章纳税。

李　杩：对不起，我是一位建筑工人，首次通关，对这点不大懂。那我应付多少税金？

安　娜：让我查一下。啊，你至少得付 100 美元。

李　杩：照章纳税是每个公民义不容辞的义务。好吧，给你税金。

安　娜：说得对。这是您的收据，请收好。检查完毕，您现在可以通行了。

李　杩：谢谢。

第二部

Formulaic Communication 日常交际习语

Asking about the Exit & Entry Border Formalities
询问有关出入境手续事宜

1. Please show me your passport/visa. 请把您的护照/签证给我看看。

   ——OK. Here's it. 好吧，这就是。

2. Where should I go through the Customs? 我该在哪里办理海关手续？

   ——The counter is over there. 那边那个柜台。

3. How much should I pay? 我该付什么关税？

   —— $ 100. 100 美元。

4. Which things are duty – free? 哪些商品免税？

   ——Except such commodities on the list. 除过这张表上的商品。

5. Are these things liable to duty? 这些东西一定要交税吗？

   ——Yes, of course. 是的，当然要交。

6. I have a *laissez – passer*. 我有免验证。

7. I've paid the duty. 我已交过税。

8. Here's the receipt. 这是收据。

第二部

Explanatory Notes注释：

1. **英语简单句（simple sentence）** 的基本句子结构是学习和提高英语口语水平应具备的起码知识，否则学习兴趣再高，学的词汇再多也不可能达到应有的目的。所以提供英语简单句下列句型，以达到夯实基础，稳步提高，循序渐进的目的。如：

   1) 主语＋不及物动词（S. + vi. / SV）。如：

   Builders work on the construction site. They'll go abroad after training English.

   2) 主语＋连系动词＋表语（S. + link v. + P. /SVP）。如：

   They're Chinese builders.　　Tom becomes a college student now.

   3) 主语＋及物动词＋宾语（S. + vt. + O. /SVO）。如：

   Builders are studying construction English, too.

   Foreigners should learn Chinese and Chinese English.

   4) 主语＋及物动词＋间接宾语＋直接宾语（S. + vt. + o. + O. / SVoO）。如：

   A foreigner teaches us architectural English every week.

   Manager Wang shows foreigners these multi-storey buildings.

   5) 主语＋及物动词＋宾语＋宾语补足语（S. + vt. + O. + o. / SVOo）。如：

   The visitors see the constructors working on the worksite.

   Electrisity makes machines run.

2. Would you mind opening your suitcase? Would you mind + doing sth. 是口语常用的句型，表示婉转的请求。Would 并不表示过去，mind 后要加带 ing 的动词。

Spoken Practice 口语练习

1. Pair Work：

Suppose you go abroad and come to the Customs. It's the first time for you to pass the Customs and you don't know anything about it. So try to say what the Customs ladies ask you to do and then what you do.

2. Tell "true" or "false" in accordance with Learn to Speak English：

1）（　　）Show me your passport when you're at the Customs.

2）（　　）At the Customs every one must show his/her visa and health certificate besides passport.

3）（　　）Passengers have to open their suitcases and briefcases for inspecting.

4）（　　）Duty free involves video camera.

5）（　　）"You're through now" means you may go into another country.

3. Read & Interpret the following Passage：

How to Form the Compounds

A girl with blue eyes is a blue-eyed girl. Children who have good looks are good-looking children. What do you call a person who is dressed well? We call him/her a well-dressed person. If the floor, wall and ceiling of a room are made so that sound can't pass through them, we should say that the room is soundproof. This is the good way to form English compounds, try to adopt this way to learn English word in your future and your glossary will be quickly extended in order to get twice the result with half the effort.

4. Fill in the Blanks with the Same Way Given and Then Learn the Following Compounds（Adjectives）by Heart：

1）ad. + a. = a.　　over-green（pine）　　_____ _____

2）n. + a. = a.　　duty-free（article）　　_____ _____

3）a. + p. p. = a.　　state-owned（enterprise）_____ _____

4）num. + n. = a.　　five-year（plan）　　_____ _____

5）n. + n. + ed. = a.　iron-willed（builder）　_____　_____

6）ad. + ving. = a.　hard-working（people）　_____　_____

7）a. + n. = a.　high-class（house）　_____　_____

8）ad. + p. p. = a.　well-known（fact）　_____　_____

9）a. + ving. = a.　good-looking（funiture）　_____　_____

5. Give Five English Sentences in accordance with the Following Sentence Patterns：

　　1）（SVO）_____.

　　2）（SVOo）_____.

　　3）（SVP）_____.

　　4）（SVoO）_____.

　　5）（SV）_____.

6. Substitute the Following Words & Expressions：

　　1）Use the following **Applying for Customs Formalities**（办理海关手续）to replace the black words in the following sentence：

　　Anna：OK. Keep good custody of it. Show me your **documents**, please.

　　安　娜：好的。保管好。请出示您的其他证件。

　　Applying for Customs Formalities［əˈplaiiŋ fəˈkʌstəmz fɔːˈmælitiz］办理海关手续

　　apply for a visa［əˈplai fə əˈviːzə］办理签证

　　entry visa［ˈentri ˈviːzə］入境签证

　　exit visa［ˈeksit ˈviːzə］出境签证

　　transit visa［ˈtrænsit ˈviːzə］过境签证

　　resident visa［ˈrezidənt ˈviːzə］居留签证

　　group visa［gruːp ˈviːzə］集体签证

　　pass［paːs］通行证

　　passport［ˈpaːspɔːt］护照

　　passport of public affairs［ˈpaːspɔːt əv ˈpʌblik əˈfeəs］公务护照

　　courier certificate［ˈkuriə səˈtifikit］信使证书

　　certificate of identity［səˈtifikit əv aiˈdentiti］身份证明书

　　identity card［aiˈdentiti kaːd］身份证

quarantine certificate［'kwɔrənti:n sə'tifikit］检疫证书

health certificate［helθ sə'tifikit］健康证

2）Use the following **Terms about Customs Inspection（海关检查相关术语）** to replace the black words in the following sentence：

Anna：Your video camera belongs to **the valuable article.** It isn't **duty free.** You have to **pay customs duty** according to regulation.

安　娜：您的摄像机属于**贵重物品**，不属**免税物**，你得按章纳税。

Terms about Customs Inspection［tə:mz ə'baut' kʌstəmz in'spekʃən］
海关检查相关术语

declaration form［ˌdeklə'reiʃən fɔ:m］申报单

traveller's cheque/check［'trævləz tʃek］旅行支票

luggage declaration［'lʌgidʒ ˌdeklə'reiʃən］行李申报单

luggage check［'lʌgidʒ tʃek］行李票/牌

hand luggage［hænd 'lʌgidʒ］随身携带行李

registered luggage［'redʒistəd 'lʌgidʒ］托运行李

customs duty［'kʌstəmz 'dju:ti］关税

duty receipt［'dju:ti ri'si:t］税单

duty-free articles［'dju:ti fri:'a:tiklz］免税物品

border checkpost［'bɔ:də 'tʃekpoust］国境检查站

Customs registration［'kʌstəmz ˌredʒis'treiʃən］海关登记

immigration office［ˌimi'greiʃən 'ɔfis］移民局

entry／exit／transit［'entri 'eksit 'trænsit］入境/出境/过境

passenger［'pæsindʒə］旅客

inspector［in'spektə］检查员

customs officer［'kʌstəmz 'ɔfisə］海关人员

Situational Dialogic Unit 11

第十一情景对话单元

Learn to Speak English

Talking about Going Abroad by Air

Anne：What time may we board the plane, Flight. 321, miss?

Alice：Let me look up the time-table for you. In two minutes.

Anne：I see. Thank you.

B. C：(after a while) Passengers for Flight 321, Beijing-Warsaw requested to board the plane now.

Betty：I'm a stewardess of this flight. 'Ready to meet guests from all over the world, ready to speed them on their ways' is our serving standard. May I see your boarding pass and ticket?

Anne：Oh, yes, here you are.

Betty：Here, take yours, please.

Anne：Thank you. Do you want to know something?

Dilys：Yes, What's the matter? Please tell me!

Anne：I'm beginning to feel a little nervous.

Dilys：There's nothing to get nervous about. You won't be nervous as usually.

Anne：I can't help being nervous. I'm a builder and this is my first trip by air, you don't know. Maybe I'm not used to go by air.

Dilys：Maybe you don't. However, there's nothing at all to worry about. Once you're up in the air, it's just like sitting at home in your own living room.

Anne：Is that so? That's just where I'd like to be right now—sitting at home in my own living room.

B. C：Passengers, welcome you to AF. Flight 321. We're taking off now. No smoking! No photos while taking off, but do fasten your safety belts.

Anne：We're in the air, right?

Dilys：Yes. Stop clenching your teeth and open your eyes. We're completely safe and sound?

学说英语

谈论乘飞机出国

安　妮：小姐，321 次班机何时可以登机？

爱丽斯：我帮你查一下时刻表。两分钟后。

安　妮：我知道啦。谢谢！

广　播：（过了一会儿）从北京飞往华沙的第 321 次班机的乘客们现在开始登机。

贝　蒂：我是这个航班的服务员，"接天下客，送万里情"是我们的服务目标。我看一下您的登记牌和机票好吗？

安　妮：哦，好吧，这就是。

贝　蒂：我核对过了。给你，请妥善保管好你的票据。

安　妮：多谢。我给你说点事好吗？

迪莉斯：好吧。什么事？请说吧。

安　妮：我已开始感到有点紧张。

迪莉斯：没什么值得紧张的，和平时一样就不紧张了。

安　妮：不由我。你不知道，我是一位建筑工人，这是我首次乘飞机出行。也许还不习惯吧。

迪莉斯：也许吧，但根本没有什么要担心的。等飞机一升到天空之后，就像在你自己家里坐在你的客厅里一样（平稳）。

安　妮：是吗？现在我真巴不得在那儿呢——坐在自己家里的客厅里。

广　播：乘客们，欢迎您搭乘我们法航第 321 次班机。我们的航班正在起飞。起飞时不许抽烟！不要拍照！但务必系好您的安全带。

安　妮：我们飞起来了，对吗？

迪莉斯：对呀。别总是咬着牙，把眼睛睁开。咱们不是安然无恙吗？

Anne: Yes. What altitude are we flying at?

Dilys: At altitude thirty thousand feet or so.

Anne: How high! What speed are we doing?

Dilys: It's now up 900 kilometres per hour (900 km/h).

Anne: According to this flying speed, I reckon our flight won't be delayed and must reach the destination on time.

Dilys: I think so. But flight is never delayed.

Anne: How long is it to arrive in Warsaw?

Dilys: Usually five hours.

Anne: oh, Five hours is to pass befor we knew it.

Dilys: Not so far. I think we're about to land in a few minutes.

Anne: What makes you think so?

Dilys: You see the plane's slowing down.

Anne: Yes, it is. My ears aren't comfortable, now a bit hurt. They just cracked terribly.

Dilys: I suppose that's the atmospheric pressure because plane is going down quickly. I've heard if you open your month and swallow hard, your ears won't crack (between swallows).

Anne: Maybe that's a good idea, Let me try. Oh, what you said has come true!

Dilys: Yes. Be a little philosophical. Nothing is going to happen to us.

Anne: I follow what you said because you've got experience by air

B. C. : Ladies and gentlemen, our plane is landing. Please fasten your safety belts. Warsaw Airport is coming about a few minutes.

Anne: OK. Landing was very smooth. Flying makes me feel happy. As travelling by air is both fast and punctual.

Dilys: I'm pleased to hear this.

安　妮：是很安全。我们现在的飞行高度是多少？

迪莉斯：大约在 3 万英尺高度航行。

安　妮：可真高呀！我们现在的飞行速度是多少？

迪莉斯：现在达到每小时 900 公里速度（900 公里／小时）。

安　妮：按照这样的速度，我估计我们不会误机，会准时抵达目的地。

迪莉斯：我想也是。飞机一般不会误机。

安　妮：到华沙要飞行多长时间？

迪莉斯：通常只需五个小时。

安　妮：啊，不知不觉五小时就要到了。

迪莉斯：不远了吧。我想飞机就要降落啦。

安　妮：何以见得？

迪莉斯：你看飞机正在减速。

安　妮：可不是吗，我的耳朵有点不舒服，现在有点痛，就是胀得厉害。

迪莉斯：我想是飞机下降得太快，大气压的缘故吧。我听人说过如果张大嘴并用力吞咽，你的耳朵就不胀了（一面咽一面说）。

安　妮：也许是个好法子，我来试试！啊，你说得还真灵验。

迪莉斯：好办法。冷静点儿，不会发生什么事的。

安　妮：你乘飞机有经验，我听你的。

广　播：女士们，先生们，本架飞机现在开始降落，请系好你们的安全带，飞机即将降落于华沙机场。

安　妮：着陆很平稳，飞行使我感到很愉快，因为乘飞机既快又准时。

迪莉斯：我很高兴听到这点。

Formulaic Communication 日常交际习语

Asking Something by Air 询问乘飞机事宜

1. On what day does plane leave for Chicago (USA)? 哪天有班机到（美国）芝加哥？

    ——On Jan. 1st. 在元月一号。

2. What flight to Geneva (Switzerland) is there in the morning? 上午有什么班机到（瑞士）日内瓦？

    ——Yes/ No. 有/没有。

3. When does the next flight leave for London (Great Britain)? 到（英国）伦敦去的下一航班何时候起飞？

    ——At eight A. M. 上午八点钟。

4. What time will the flight arrive in Madrid (Spain)? 航班何时抵达（西班牙）马德里？

    ——At seven P. M. 下午七点钟。

5. Where does the flight stop on the way to Paris (France)? 飞机到（法国）巴黎沿线在什么地方停？

    ——Moscow. 莫斯科。

6. Where is Sydney (Australia) -Shanghai (China) Plane? 从（澳大利亚）悉尼飞往（中国）上海的班机在哪儿？

    ——Over there. 就在那边。

7. What time am I suppose to check in? 我何时应办登机手续？

    ——An hour later according to timetable. 根据时刻表，一小时后。

8. How much luggage can one take on the plane? 一个人可以带多重的行李？

    ——Ten kilogram according to the regulation，根据规定，10公斤。

9. How much should I pay for the overweight? 我应付多少超重行李费

    ——Five Yuan is OK. 五元钱就可以了。

10. to miss the train/ship/plane 误车/船/飞机

11. to meet sb. 接某人

12. to see sb. off 送某人

13. sea/air/car trainsick 晕船/机/车/火车

Explanatory Notes注释：

一般疑问句（**General Question**）是口语会话中使用频率较高的句子，为了提高口语会话水平，掌握好其特点，有必要进一步强调下列几点。例如：

1. 一般疑问句就是由动词 be, have 或助动词，情态动词开头用于证实情况，由 Yes 或 No 来回答。一般疑问句还分肯定句和否定句两种，这一单元先讲肯定句。一般疑问句读声调"↗"。

2. 一般肯定疑问句的句型是 **be**, **have** 或助动词，情态动词 + 主语 + 动词 + ?。如：

   Are you all new stutends ↗? Yes, we are/No, we aren't.

   Do you study Architectural English ↗? Yes, we do/No, we don't.

3. 一般疑问句问句使用的动词和答语使用的动词不同。如：

   1）**Need** I help you? 要我帮帮你吗？

      Yes, you **must**. 是的，要帮助

      No, you **needn't**. 不，不必。

   2）**Must** we aid you? 我们要援助你吗？

      Yes, you must. 是的，你们必须援助。

      No, you **needn't**. 不，你们**不必**。

   3）**May** I photo here? 我可以在此拍照吗？

      I don't think you **can**. 我想不能。

      May I come in your construction site to see Chinese builders how to build the buildings?

      我可以进到你们施工现场看看中国建筑工人是怎样盖楼的吗？

      No, you **mustn't**. 不，**不行**。

【注】mustn't 表示"不应该""不许可""不行"；needn't 则表示"不必"，所以 must 的否定回答一定得用 neen't；may 的否定回答一定得用 mustn't 回答，否则均视为错。

Spoken Practice口语练习

1. Pair Work：

Imagine that A is a passenger, B is one of stewardess of a plane, B tries to tell the passengers just like A what the passengers must pay attention to if the plane is up and down.

2. Tell "true" or "false" in accordance with Learn to Speak English：

1）（　　）The time-table says that we're going to board the plane, Flight No. 321 in two minutes.

2）（　　）Every lady, a stewardess of this plane has right to check passengers boarding card and ticket.

3）（　　）When the plane is up and down, passengers must fasten the seat belts.

4）（　　）The plane's about to take off that means the plane's going down.

5）（　　）The landing was very smooth. Flying makes me happy.

3. Read & Interpret the Following passage：

How to Use Mr. Mrs. Miss. Ms. and even Madam, Sir

Almost everybody knows the meanings of Mr. = Mister, Mrs. = Mistress, Miss, Ms. and even Madam, Sir. But how to use and pronounce them perhaps is unfamiliar.

Mrs. = Mistress is woman surname before she married and pronounce ['misiz]. Before the surnames of men, we choose Mr/Mister and pronounce ['mistə]. For the single woman uses Miss and pronounce [mis]. The word Mr./Mister doesn't tell us whether or not a man is married. Many women think this is an advantage for mankind. They want to be equal to men in the way. These women feel it unnecessary for people to know whether they are married or not. Today, many women prefer to use Ms. and pronounce [miz] rather than Mrs or Miss.

They're four English words to be used above-mentioned. However, sir is used to address man and madam women, both words are without first and second name. But people often say "dear sir/madam" is OK.

4. Fill in the Blanks and Then Learn the Following Compounds (Verbs) by Heart：

1) ad. + v. = v.　　overcome (difficulty)　_____　_____

2) n. + v. = v.　　safeguard (friend)　_____　_____

3) a. + v. = v.　　white-wash (walls)　_____　_____

4) prep. + v. = v.　understand (meaning)　_____　_____

5. Turn the Following into Negatives, General Questions and then Give Response if necessary：

1) Builders continue constructing on the worksite in the rainy days.

2) Manager Wang asks me to buy an air ticket for him.

3) We're Chinese constructors now.

4) Some of them have been abroad many a time in recent year.

5) The monitor of Industrial and Civil Class has got something to tell us right now.

6) I may give you my advance after work.

7) The large bridge over the wide river was built by Chinese Building Engineering Company last century.

8) There're many high and big beautiful buildings on both sides of the trees in the city.

9) Xiao Hai needs some help at the moment.

10) Chief engineer are talking about this year's production plan to some managing staff in the meeting room on the twenty floor of his multi-storey office building.

6. Substitute the Following Words & Expressions：

1) Use the following **Terms about Airport** (机场相关术语) to replace the black words in the following sentence：

Anne：OK. **Landing** was very smooth. **Flying** makes me feel happy. As travelling by **air** is both fast and punctual.

安　妮：**着陆**很平稳，**飞行**使我感到很愉快，因为乘飞机既快又准时。

Terms about Airport [tə:mz ə'baut 'ɛəpɔ:t] 机场相关术语

terminal building ['tə:minl 'bildiŋ] 候机楼

control tower [kən'troul 'tauə] 指挥塔

runway ['rʌnwei] 跑道

ramp [ræmp] 旋梯

armchair seat ['a:m'tʃɛə si:t] 座椅

airline ticket ['ɛəlain 'tikit] 机票

boarding card ['bɔ:diŋ ka:d] 登记牌

check in [tʃek in] 办理报到手续

free luggage [fri:'lʌgidʒ] 免税行李

excess luggage [ik'ses 'lʌgidʒ] 超重行李

take off [teik ɔ(:)f] 起飞

climbing ['klaimiŋ] 爬行

landing ['lændiŋ] 降落

touch down ['tʌtʃdaun] 着地

2）Use the following **Flight Crew and Others**（机组人员和其他）to replace the black words in the following sentence：

Betty：I'm a **stewardess** of this plane. 'Ready to meet guests from all over the world, ready to speed them on their ways' is our serving standard. May I see your **boarding pass** and **ticket**?

贝　蒂：我是这个航班的**服务员**，"接天下客，送万里情"是我们的服务目标。我看一下您的登记牌和机票好吗？

Flight Crew and Others [flait kru:ənd 'ʌθəz] 机组人员和其他人员

steward ['stjuəd] 男服务员

stewardess ['stjuədis] 女服务员

pilot ['pailət] 驾驶员

flyer ['flaiə] 飞行员

navigator ['nævigeitə] 领航员

passenger ['pæsindʒə] 旅客，乘客

civil aircraft ['sivl 'ɛəkra:ft] 民航飞机

passenger plan ['pæsindʒə plæn] 客机

airliner ['ɛə,lainə] 班机

Situational Dialogic Unit 12

第十二情景对话单元

Learn to Speak English

Talking about Asking the Way

A

Stranger: Excuse me, please tell me the way to the Embassy of the P. R. C?

Jackson: Oh. Turn to left at the first lights and then take Bus No. 2 till the end. I don't think you can miss it.

Stranger: I see. Will it take me long time to get there?

Jackson: No, it's no distance at all, probably half an hour is enough.

Stranger: Many thanks, sir.

Jackson: Not at all.

B

Stranger: Sorry to disturb you. I'm a Chinese builder and have just arrived here. I don't know where, which direction it is the Head Office of CSCEC?

Dampier: Sorry. I'm afraid I can't. I'm new around here, too.

Stranger: Well, thank you any way.

Caroline: I can help you, sir. I couldn't overhear you ask the way. I'm a local and know here like the back of my hand.

Stranger: That's great! How to go, Ms? Please tell me right now.

Caroline: Take the third road on the right and go straight on.

Stranger: How far is it from here, Ms?

Caroline: Not so far. Maybe half a kilometre. No need to take any bus, it takes you about ten minutes on foot.

Stranger: Thank you for taking so much trouble in directing me. Or I must waste too much time and walk a long way.

Caroline: That's quite all right. It's completely easy.

学说英语

谈论问路

A

陌生者：劳驾，请告诉我到中华人民共和国大使馆怎么走？

杰克逊：啊，走到第一排红绿灯处向左拐，然后乘2路公共汽车直到终点。我想你不会迷路的。

陌生者：我明白啦。要花费我很长时间到哪儿吗？

杰克逊：不用，一点儿也不远。也许半个小时就到了。

陌生者：多谢啦，先生。

杰克逊：不客气。

B

陌生者：对不起，打扰你一下。我是一位中国建筑工人，初来乍到，我不知道中建总部在哪儿？该走哪个方向？

丹皮尔：对不起，我恐怕帮不了你这个忙，我对这儿也很生疏。

陌生者：啊，那也得谢谢你。

卡罗琳：先生，我能帮你的忙，我无意中听到你问去中建总部的路。我是当地人，对这儿了如指掌。

陌生者：那可太好啦！该怎么走呢？女士，请快告诉我吧。

卡罗琳：你走到第三条马路时右转弯一直走就是。

陌生者：女士，离这儿有多远？

卡罗琳：不多远，也许0.5公里。不需乘车，步行大约10多分钟就能到。

陌生者：真该多谢你给我指路，要不然我不知会浪费多少时间，走多少冤枉路。

卡罗琳：那没什么。这完全是举手之劳。

Formulaic Communication 日常交际习语

Asking the Way and Responses 问路与应答

1. How can I get to the city center? I don't know the way. 我不认识路，请问去市中心怎么走？

——Go down this street. 沿着这条街走。

2. Is this the right way to Eastern Street? 到东大街是从这儿走吗？

——Yes, it is. 是的。

3. Which is the nearest/ best way to the railway station? 哪条是到火车站最近/好的路？

——This way. 这条路。

4. Excuse me. Can you tell me the way to Hilton Hotel? 劳驾，你能告诉我去希尔顿饭店的路吗？

——Certainly. Turn right/left at first/second crossing. 肯定能。在第一/二个十字路口向右/ 左拐就到了。

Explanatory Notes注释：

1. I'm **new** around here, too. 我对这儿也很生疏。New 的意思是 strange 陌生，不熟悉：New 还有 Haven't any experirce 没经验的意思。如：She's new to the work. 他对这项工作缺乏经验。

2. 选择疑问句（**Alternative Question**）就是提出两种情况供对方选择的一种疑问句。句型是"**一般疑问句 + or + 一般疑问句（省掉意义上与前句相同部分）+?**"，这种句子要求直接回答，决不能出现 Yes/No。在读时应注意，前一疑问句读升调"↗"，而后一疑问句则读降调"↘"。如：

   1）Will you go to visit the workshop ↗ or worksite ↘ this afternoon? (I'll go to visit) the worksite ↘ (this afternoon.)

   2）Do you study building decoration ↗ or construction accounting ↘? (We study) building decoration. ↘

   3）Is your sister a middle school student ↗ or a college student ↘? (She's) a college student. ↘

第二部

Spoken Practice 口语练习

1. Pair Work：

Suppose you're a stranger in the country and doesn't know the way to Com-plant (中成公司) and how to go，so have to ask a local person whom you meet. Try to say how you should begin asking and how you can get to the place where you want to go.

2. Tell "true" or "false" in accordance with Learn to Speak English

1) (　　　) I spent a long time to reach the Embassy of the P. R. C.

2) (　　　) You should turn right at first lights and then take Bus No. 2 till the end.

3) (　　　) I'm afraid I'm also a new comer here，I don't know either.

4) (　　　) Please take the third block on the right and go straight on.

5) (　　　) Thank you for taking so much trouble in showing me.

3. Read & Interpret the Following Passage：

Asking for Directions

　　People are usually helpful if you ask for directions. But you should have the exact address and as specific as possible. Although all houses have a street number，many are known only by a name. If you have difficulty in finding such house，telephone directories are the most common source of addresses. Remember that many cities and some towns are usually built in blocks. For example，people will often tell strangers to "go one or two blocks and turn left".

4. Interpret the Following Expressions and Answer Them If Possible：

1) Which directions is it to 建设工程部？

2) Can you tell me the way to 中国大使馆 in the country？

3) Could you direct me to ... 建筑科技大学？

4) Would you tell me how to get to 中国建筑总公司非洲办事处？

5) Please show me where is 经理办公室？

5. Make Some Alternative Questions with the Words Given and then Gave them Answer：

1）worksite, factory

_____? _____.

2）study, teach

_____? _____.

3）a middle school student, a college student

_____? _____.

4）Beijing, Shanghai

_____? _____.

5）right, left

_____? _____.

6. Substitute the Following Words & Expressions：

1）Use the following **Building Managing Units**（建筑管理单位）to replace the black words in the following sentence：

Stranger：Sorry to disturb you. I'm a Chinese builder and have just arrived here. I don't know where, which direction it is **the Head Office of CSCEC**?

陌生者：对不起，打扰你一下。我是一位中国建筑工人，初来乍道，我不知到**中建总部**在哪儿？该走哪个方向？

Buiding Managing Units ［ˈbildiŋ ˈmænidʒiŋ ˈjuːnits］建筑管理单位

Building Designing Institute ［ˈbildiŋ diˈzainiŋ ˈinstitjuːt］建筑设计院

Architectural Institute ［ˌɑːkiˈtektʃərəl ˈinstitjuːt］建筑学会

Institute of Architects ［ˈinstitjuːt əv ˈɑːkitekts］建筑师学会

Building Office ［ˈbildiŋ ˈɔfis］建筑事务所

The State building Commission ［ðə steit ˈbildiŋ kəˈmiʃən］国家建设委员会

The Ministry of Building Engineering ［ðə ˈministri əv ˈbildiŋ ˌendʒiˈniəriŋ］建设工程部

Urban & Rural Planning Association ［ˈəːbən ənd ˈruərəl ˈplæniŋ əˌsousiˈeiʃən］城乡规划协会

Construction Quality Supervision Station ［kənˈstrʌkʃən ˈkwɔliti ˌsjuː

pə'viʒən 'steiʃən] 建筑质量监督站

Civil Construction Engineering Institute ['sivl kən'strʌkʃən ˌendʒi'niəriŋ 'institjuːt] 土木建筑工程学会

2） Use the following **Position and Direction**（方位与方向）to replace the black words in the following sentence：

Jackson：Oh. **Turn to left** at the first lights and then take Bus No. 2 till **the end.** I don't think you can miss it.

杰克逊：啊。到第一排红绿灯处**向左拐，**然后乘 2 路公共汽车直到 **终点。**我想你不会迷路的。

Position and Direction [pə'ziʃən ənd di'rekʃən] 方位与方向

east [iːst] 东　　　　　　　　southeast ['sauθ'iːst] 东南

west [west] 西　　　　　　　　northeast ['nɔː'θ'iːst] 东北

south [sauθ] 南　　　　　　　　southwest ['sauθ'west] 西南

north [nɔːθ] 北　　　　　　　　northwest ['nɔːθ'west] 西北

right [rait] 右边　　　　　　　　left [left] 左边

front [frʌnt] 前面　　　　　　　back [bæk] 后面

block [blɔk] 街坊　　　　　　　district ['distrikt] 地区

Situational Dialogic Unit 13

第十三情景对话单元

Learn to Speak English

Talking about Riding a bus or Taking a Taxi

Liuxin: Does the bus go to Complant Office?

Driver: No. You're going to the wrong way. You have to get off at the next stop and change Bus No. 8.

Liuxin: Take Bus No. 8. I see. Thanks. (After few minutes) Is the Bus No. 8 to Complant Office, miss?

Driver: Yes. Please come along, hurry up.

Liuxin: Thanks. How much is a fare?

Driver: 50 C. Just drop your money into the box.

Liuxin: OK. I'm a stranger here. Please tell me when I get to Complant Office, right?

Driver: All right. I'll remind you when it's your stop. (Half an hour later). Here you are. Sorry, my bus stops here because this is its terminus therefore you have to take a taxi.

Liuxin: Thank you. (After few minutes) Hey, taxi!

Driver: Hello, please get on, sir. Where do you want to go?

Liuxin: Complant Office. Do you have any idea what the fare will be? I'd love to know.

Driver: Probably $ 10. It may cost you more than or less than ten cents. I can't tell exactly. But whatever it is, it'll show on the meter.

Liuxin: Are you quite sure it won't be any more?

Driver: Certainly not. (After ten minutes) Here you are, sir. The meter says $ 9. 80.

Liuxin: OK. Here's ten.

Driver: All right, sir. Here's your change.

Liuxin: Keep to your change. Bye!

Driver: You're too kind. Thank you. Goodbye!

学说英语

谈论乘公共汽车还是搭出租车

刘　欣：这辆（公共汽）车通往中成办事处吗？

司　机：不。您搭错车了，您得在下一站下车再换乘 8 路车。

刘　欣：乘 8 路车。我明白啦。谢谢！（过了一会儿）小姐，8 路车通往中成办事处吗？

司　机：是的。请快点，赶紧上车吧！

刘　欣：谢谢！票价是多少？

司　机：50 美分。把钱投进投币箱就是了。

刘　欣：好的。我对这儿不熟悉，车到中成办事处时，请告诉我一声好吗？

司　机：好的，车到站时，我会提醒您的。（半小时后）您到站啦。对不起，我的车不往前走了，这是终点站，您得换乘出租车。

刘　欣：多谢。（过了一会儿）喂，出租车！

司　机：你好，先生，请上车。你想到哪儿？

刘　欣：中成办事处。我想知道得花多少车费？

司　机：大约 10 美元吧。可能会多或少十几美分，我也说不准。不管多少钱，（里程收费）表上都会显出来的。

刘　欣：你肯定不会再多了吗？

司　机：当然不会。（过了十分钟）您到了，先生。计价器显示 9.80 美元。

刘　欣：好吧。这是 10 元钱。

司　机：好的，先生。这是给您找的钱。

刘　欣：不用找了。再见！

司　机：你太客气啦。谢谢！走好！

Formulaic Communication 日常交际习语

Asking Something by Bus and Responses 询问乘公共汽车事宜与应答

1. Does this bus go to Building Designing Institute? 这路车去不去建筑设计院?

   ——Ye, it is. 是的,去。/No, it is not. 不,不去。

2. How often does Bus 206 run? 206 路车多长时间一趟?

   ——The bus runs about every 5 minutes. 这路车大约 5 分钟一趟。

3. How many stops to Construction Engineering Vocational College? 到建筑工程职业学院有几站?

   ——ten stops. 10 站。

4. Which bus should I take for The Ministry of building Engineering? 我要到建筑工程部该乘哪路公共汽车?

   ——(You should) take Bus No. 6. (你应)乘 6 路车。

5. Is it far to walk after I get out? 下车后我还得走很远吗?

   ——Not very far. It's about five minutes' walk. 不太远。步行约 5 分钟的路程。

6. Please let me know when to get off. What's the next stop? 请告诉我什么时候下车。下一站是什么站?

   —— This is your stop. Bell Tower Stop. 你到站了。钟楼站。

7. What's the fare? 车票多少钱?

   ——One yuan, please. 请付 1 元。

8. This is your stop. 您到站了。

9. Get in, please. 请上车。

10. All change now. 都下车。

11. You've missed your stop. 你坐过站了。

12. You've taken the wrong bus. You have to get off at the next stop and take Bus No. 689. 你乘错了车。你得下一站下车换乘 689 路车。

Explanatory Notes注释：

1. **反义疑问句（Disjunctiontive Question）** 是英语口语会话常用的问句。这种问句附在陈述句后并对陈述事实提出疑问，用 Yes 或 No 来回答。该句分两部分，第一部分为陈述句用"，"读降调"↘"，第二部分为疑问句用"?"，表示疑问时读升调"↗"，加强语气时则读降调"↘"。为了更好的运用反义疑问句，应掌握该句的下列三种句型。

   句型 I　主语 + 肯定谓语 + 其他，否定谓语 + 主语?
   　　　　Yes，主语 + 肯定谓语。　 No，主语 + 否定谓语。 如：
   1）The man over there is a local builder, isn't he? Yes, he is/No, he isn't.
   2）They work on the building site, don't they? Yes, they do/No, they don't.

   句型 II　主语 + 否定谓语 + 其他，肯定谓语 + 主语?
   　　　　Yes，主语 + 肯定谓语　No，主语 + 否定谓语。 如：
   1）She doesn't teach you Chinese, does she?
   　　Yes, she does.（不，她是。）**No**, she doesn't.（是，她不是。）
   2）The boy isn't freshman, is he?
   　　Yes, he is.（不，他是。）**No**, he isn't.（是，他不是。）

   句型 III　特殊的反义疑问句，应注意疑问部分的谓语动词变化。 如：
   1）He used to live in Bejing, **usedn't** he/**didn't** he?
   2）Those students ought not to be punished, **ought** they?
   3）That girl is hardly 18 years old, **is** she?
   4）I'm late this time, **ain't** I?
   5）Let's go to see the new buildings, **shall** we?
   6）Let us look at your tools, **will** you?
   7）Let's not go shopping after class, **all right/ OK**?

2. 有关搭乘出租车/计程车的习惯说法：go by taxi / go in taxi 乘计程车去，get in（into）a taxi 上计程车，get out of a taxi 下计程车。

Spoken Practice口语练习

1. Pair Work：

A acts as an American, B acts as a Chinese builder who just comes out of an American Airport and really doesn't know which direction Complant construction site is. B meets A and asks A how far the site is and how to get there, and bus or taxi which is better for B to take.

2. Tell "true" or "false" in accordance with Learn to Speak English：

1) (   ) Passengers pay according to the meter if they take bus.

2) (   ) Just drop 50 C into the box when you get on a taxi.

3) (   ) I'll tell you where you get on.

4) (   ) You have to take a car. My bus won't get there.

5) (   ) Here is ten. Keep to your small money.

3. Read & Interpret the Following Passage：

What Is the Meter?

The meter is a device in the taxi. Whenever the taxi starts out with passenger, the flag is put up and that the meter starts its function. The meter registers the distance and shows the exact amount of the fare. The passenger pays the taxi driver according to it. Today all the taxies have already equipped such meters. It's clear and reasonable for the passengers to pay.

4. Give the Full Form of the Following Contractions or the Abbreviated Form of the Full Words：

the Full Form of the Example：   I've = （I have）

1) You'd better go = （   )   4) doesn't = （   )

2) There're = （   )   5) She'd like to = （   )

3) You'd better go = （   )   6) shouldn't = （   )

the Abbreviated Form of the Example：（don't） = do not

7) (   ) = He is /He has   9) (   ) = There is

8) (   ) = cannot/can not   10) (   ) = will not

5. Put the Following into Chinese or English and then Answer Them：

1）Manager Wang used to live in America, didn't he?

_____, _____?

2）I'm late this time, ain't I?

_____, _____?

3）Let us look at your new dictionary, will you?

_____, _____?

4）That student is hardly 18 years old, is she?

_____, _____?

5）Let's go to see the new buildings, shall we?

_____, _____?

6）咱们下午不上英语课，对吗?

_____, _____?

7）施工人员下个周末继续上班，不是吗?

_____, _____?

8）那边那位小伙子是大一的新生，是吗?

_____, _____?

9）工民建班的学生明年春季不去实习，不是吗?

_____, _____?

10）中国工人，你们该下车了，对吗?

_____, _____?

6. Substitute the Following Words & Expressions：

1）Use the following **Terms about Traffic**（交通相关词语）to replace the black words in the following sentence：

Driver: No. You're going to the wrong way. You have to get off at the next **stop** and change **the Bus No. 8.**

司　机：不。您搭错车了，您得在下一站下车再换乘 **8 路车**。

Terms about Traffic［ˈtɜːmz əˈbaut ˈtræfik］交通相关词语

traffic map［ˈtræfik mæp］交通图

street［striːt］街道

crossing［ˈkrɔsiŋ］交叉路口

block［blɔk］街区

corner［'kɔ·nə］拐角

pavement［'peivmənt］人行道

traffic lights［'træfik laits］交通信号灯

traffic signal［'træfik 'signəl］交通信号

traffic jam［'træfik dʒæm］交通阻塞

police box［pə'li;s bɔks］警亭

safety island［'seifti 'ailənd］安全岛

highroad［'hairoud］公路（英）

highway［'haiwei］公路

expressway［iks'preswei］高速公路

2）Use the following **Terms about Bus and Taxi（公共汽车和出租车 相关词语）** to replace the black words in the following sentence：

Liuxin：Thank you.（After few minutes）Hey，**taxi**！

刘　欣：多谢。（过了一会儿）喂，**出租车**！

Terms about Bus and Taxi［tə;mz ə'baut bʌs ənd'tæksi］公共汽车 和出租车相关词语

taxi stand［'tæksi stænd］出租车站

bus stop［bʌs stɔp］公共汽车站

the next stop［ðə nekst stɔp］下一站

the nearest stop［ðə 'niərist stɔp］最近的车站

fare［fɛə］车费

ticket［'tikit］车票

conductor［kən'dʌktə］售票员

driver［'draivə］司机，驾驶员

stopping［'stɔpiŋ］停车

speeding up［'spi;diŋ ʌp］加速

slowing down［'slouiŋ daun］减速

backing；reversing［'bækiŋ ri'və;siŋ］倒车

turning left/right［'tə;niŋ left rait］向左/右

Situational Dialogic Unit 14

第十四情景对话单元

Learn to Speak English

Talking about Taking a Train or an Underground

Sunsi：Would you please tell me why the two English words 'Underground and Subway' are the same meaning and what's the difference between them?

Anne：Oh, There's no difference at all, and the only difference is Britain English and American English.

Sunsi：Which word is British English and which is American, please tell me, OK?

Anne：No problem. Underground is British English, and subway is American.

Sunsi：My English is poor. I asked such simple question that makes you laugh at me.

Anne：That's OK. As you're a foreigner and English isn't your native language, I know you. learning language needs not feeling ashamed to ask and learning from one's subordinates and then can improve it.

Sunsi：Sound reseanable. As a matter of fact, I learn and improve English with this attitude.

Anne：Yours is fine and makes me admire, but you must hold on your own action.

Sunsi：All right. I must study assiduously and perseveringly. By the way, I'm going to China-town, and which should I take there, a train or an underground, sir?

Anne：Train is better, I think.

Sunsi：But why not underground, sir?

Anne：Because the train is both fast and economy.

Sunsi：You're right. Which train?

Anne：Train No. 369. It starts at 9∶15 from the platform 20.

Sunsi：When does it get there?

Anne：It takes roughly three hours so you'll be·there before one P. M.

学说英语

谈论乘火车还是坐地铁

孙　思：请您告诉我为什么"Underground 和 Subway"这两个英语单词意思一样，有什么不同之处吗？

安　妮：啊，没什么不同之处，只是英国英语和美国英语用词不同而已。

孙　思：哪个词是英语用法，哪个词是美语用法，请告诉我好吗？

安　妮：没问题。Underground 是英语用法，Subway 则是美语用法。

孙　思：我的英语很差，问这么简单的问题让你见笑啦。

安　妮：没什么。我可以理解，因为你是外国人，英语不是你的母语。再说学习语言就是要不耻下问，才能有所提高。

孙　思：言之有理，其实我就是抱着这种态度学习英语的。

安　妮：你这种态度可嘉，令我敬佩，但贵在坚持呀。

孙　思：对。我一定刻苦学习，持之以恒。顺便问一下去唐人街，我该乘火车还是乘地铁，先生？

安　妮：我想最好乘火车。

孙　思：那为什么不乘地铁呢，先生？

安　妮：因为火车既快又便宜么。

孙　思：说的对。乘哪次车？

安　妮：369 次车。这趟车 9：15 在第 20 站台发车。

孙　思：何时可以到达？

安　妮：路上大约要花三个小时，所以您到那儿正好是在下午一点之前。

Sunsi: That's good. Is it necessary to change?

Anne: No, it's a through train

Sunsi: What's the fare, please?

Anne: Do you like to buy the single trip ticket or round trip ticket, I have to know, sir?

Sunsi: Oh, sorry. What's the difference between the two, miss?

Anne: Sure. A round trip ticket saves you about 10% of fare.

Sunsi: Naturally, a round trip ticket. This is money for ticket.

Anne: Your money is just well and needn't any change. This is your ticket and takes care of it, please.

Sunsi: Many thanks for your help.

B. C: All a board, please! The Train No. 369 is to start.

孙　思：那好。还要转车吗？

安　妮：不需要，这是一趟直达车。

孙　思：请问票价是多少？

安　妮：先生，我得知道您打算买单程票还是往返票？

孙　思：啊，对不起，小姐，这两种票有什么不同吗？

安　妮：肯定有。往返票比单程票可以节省百分子之十（10％）的车费。

孙　思：那自然就买一张往返票。给你票钱。

安　妮：钱正好，不需找。这是你的车票，请保管好。

孙　思：多谢你的关照。

广　播：各位旅客，请上车！369 次列车就要开车啦。

Formulaic Communication 日常交际习语

Asking Something at the Railway/Subway Station and Responses
在火车/地铁站询问事宜与应答

1. Is this a through train or express train? 这是一趟直达车还是一趟快车？
   —— (It's an) express train. （是）趟快车。

2. Shall I have to change the train if I take this train? 我要不要再转车，假如我乘这趟车的话？
   ——Yes, I think so. 是的，我想是。

3. Is this a right plateform for Paris train? 到巴黎的车从这个站台上车是吗？
   ——Yes, it's right platform. 对，就在这个站台上。

4. What time is the next train for New York? 去纽约下趟车何时开？
   ——After ten minutes. 10分钟后。

5. Is there any other train to get to London? 还有别的车可以到伦敦去吗？
   ——No. this is only one. 没有。这是唯一一趟火车。

6. Is this a through train? 这是趟直达车吗？
   ——Yes, it is. 是的。

7. Shall I have to change it anywhere? 我还得在什么地方转车吗？
   ——No, you won't. 不，不倒。

8. The train/ship leaves at 18.00 p. m. 开车/船的时间是下午6点钟。

9. I've to catch the train/ bus 我得赶火车/汽车。

Explanatory Notes注释：

1. '地铁' 这一词，除了英国人的叫法 Underground，美国人的用法 subway 外，其实还有 metro［'metrou］（colloq. Abbrev. of）the metropolitan railway（俗）地下铁道（是 metropolitan railway 的略语）。

2. get on（onto）上车，get off 下车（也可用于上/下公共汽车或火车）。

3. **But why not underground, sir**? 是 but why won't you take an underground, sir? 的省略句，也是一种特殊疑问句。特殊疑问句是英语口语中使用率很高的问句，因此有必要对其进一步强调。

   特殊疑问句（Special Question） 其实就是对句中某一部分提问的疑问句，所以就得用疑问词（interrogative）。疑问词包括疑问代词（interrogative pronouns），如：what、who、whom、whose、which，用于作除了状语外的句子成分；疑问副词（interrogative adverbs）如：when、why、where、how，只能用作状语。所以答语要针对句中问题直接回答，读降调 "↘"，常用的句型有下列三种。如：

   1）**疑问词 + 一般疑问句**（疑问词作宾语、表语、状语或定语）+ ？例如：

      Who/whom are you looking for?（I'm looking for）my manager.

      What do you do on the site?（We）paint the wall.

   2）**疑问代词（+ 名词）+ 谓语**（疑问代词作主语或主语的定语时，用陈述句的语序）+ ？例如：

      Which is better, the direct method of teaching English or the comparative?

      The comparative.

      Who teaches your English? Tom.

   3）**疑问词 + 一般否定疑问句**（表示劝告、建议、责备等）+ ？例如：

      Why didn't you go to work? Because I was ill.

Spoken Practice 口语练习

1. Pair Work：

Suppose you're a Chinese building worker in a large city and don't know how to go to your new construction site, you should take a train or an underground, after you ask a policeman whom you meet. Try to say what you should begin asking and a train or an underground which is better for you to take.

2. Tell "true" or "false" in accordance with Learn to Speak English：

1）（　　） It's much better for me to take a taxi to China-town.

2）（　　） Taking a subway to the head office of CSCEC is both fast and economy.

3）（　　） It takes about three hours so you'll be there before two P. M.

4）（　　） Train ticket fare of single trip and return trip are same price.

5）（　　） According to Train Time-table, train No. 369 starts at 9：15 from the platform 20.

3. Read & Interpret the following Passage：

The Underground

There're underground systems in several large cities in the world today, they've an extensive and rather complicated rapid transit systems so that passengers go to take them conveniently. Each train is designated by letter or a number for the passengers to see. Fares on underground aren't fixed at all, but are proportional to the distance travelled. Passengers must have a ticket or, in some cases, the exact charge to get on the platforms.

4. Read the Following Special Compounds and Then Learn Them by Heart：

1）nothing-can-be-done（attitude）　　无法可想的（态度）

2）good-for-nothing（material）　　不中用的（材料）

3）face-to-face（talk）　　面对面的（谈话）

4）happy-go-lucky（work）   无忧无虑的（工作）

5）over-all（plan）   总的（计划）

6）up-to-date（machine）   新式的（机器）

7）wait-and-see   走着瞧

8）hide-and-seek   捉迷藏

9）go-between   中间人

10）by-product   副产品

5. Make the Special Questions in Accordance with the Following *Italics*（斜体字）every part：

The young man/is studying/moden building materials/in an architectural collage/now.

1）Who _____ ?

2）What _____ ?

3）Where _____ ?

4）When _____ ?

Chinese builders/contract and construct/more than 100 projects/abroad/in a year.

5）Which _____ ?

6）What _____ ?

7）How many _____ ?

8）Where _____ ?

9）How long _____ ?

6. Substitute the Following Words & Expressions：

1）Use the following **Terms about Underground**（地铁相关术语）to replace the black words in the following sentence：

Sunsi：But why not **Underground**, sir?

孙　思：那为什么不乘**地铁**呢，先生？

Terms about Underground ［ˈtəːmz əˈbaut ˈʌndəɡraund］地铁相关术语

terminus ［ˈtəːminəs］终点站

platform ［ˈplætfɔːm］站台

circle line ［ˈsəːkl lain］环形线路

information desk [ˌinfəˈmeiʃən desk] 问讯处

escalator [ˈeskəleitə] 电动扶梯

entrance/exit [ˈentrəns ˈeksit] 入／出口

electric train [iˈlektrik trein] 电力机车

carriage [ˈkæridʒ] 车厢

2）Use the following **Terms about Train**（火车相关术语）to replace the black words in the following sentence：

Anne：**Train** is better, I think.

安妮：我想最好乘**火车**。

Terms about Train [təːmz əˈbaut trein] **火车相关术语**

express [iksˈpres] 快车

special express [ˈspeʃəl iksˈpres] 特快车

through express [θruː iksˈpres] 直达快车

single ticket [ˈsiŋgl ˈtikit] 单程票

return ticket [riˈtəːn ˈtikit] 往返（程）票

half ticket [haːf ˈtikit] 半票

railway timetable [ˈreilwei ˈtaimˌteibl] 火车时刻表

booking office [ˈbukiŋ ˈɔfis] 售票处

way station [wei ˈsteiʃən] 中途站

railway station [ˈreilwei ˈsteiʃən] 火车站

tunnel [ˈtʌnl] 隧道／洞

railway bridge [ˈreilwei bridʒ] 铁路桥

Situational Dialogic Unit 15

第十五情景对话单元

Learn to Speak English

Talking about Staying at a Hotel

Jones: This is the **Weeks Hotel**, welcome you.

Luna: Thank you. Do you have four single rooms? Or if you have two double-beded rooms, so much the better.

Jones: Sorry. We're practically full up, but I'll see. How long do you intend to stay, sir?

Luna: We're Chinese. We come here to tender the construction George Airport, so we expect to stay here for a week at least.

Jones: I see. You can have a double – beded room on the first floor, room 108, and two single rooms on the twentieth, room 2005 and 2006.

Luna: That's all right. But what's rate per day, please?

Jones: Our hotel is 3 – star hotel. So all the outside rooms with bath are fifty Marks and up per day.

Luna: I don't suppose you have any cheaper rooms?

Jones: Yes. I can give you two inside rooms without bath at thirty marks. They're on the top floor and have plenty of air and light.

Luna: OK, we're on business. Does the rate include meals?

Jones: Yes. Just breakfast and supper. There're both Chinese and Western food there. Guests can freely choose the food to have according to their life habits and customs.

Luna: That's fine. What food?

Jones: Rice, bread, noodles and so forth.

Luna: Drinks, miss?

Jones: Coffee, tea, milk and mineral water, you can drink anything as you like.

Luna: I see. Which floor is the dining hall on, miss?

Jones: It's at the eastern end of the ground floor. You can have meals at your rooms or in the hall.

Luna: That's not bad, nice and good, I think.

学说英语

谈论在饭店/旅馆居住

琼　斯：这是**威克斯饭店**，欢迎光临。

卢　娜：谢谢！能给我们提供四个单人房间吗？如果有两套双人床房间，那就再好不过啦！

琼　斯：对不起，差不多已住满了，不过我再查看一下。先生，你们打算住多久呀？

卢　娜：我们是中国人，我们前来此地是要投乔治机场的施工标。所以我们打算在此至少居住一个星期。

琼　斯：我知道啦！给你们安排的双人床房间在二楼，108 房间；两个单人房间在第二十层，2005 和 2006 房间。

卢　娜：那就好。请问每天需付多少钱？

琼　斯：我们的饭店是三星级饭店。所有靠外侧带洗澡间的房间每天 50 马克或 50 马克以上。

卢　娜：不知你们还有没有便宜一点儿的房间？

琼　斯：有。我可以给你们提供两个靠马路不带洗澡间的房间，每天 30 马克，那是顶层，阳光和空气都很充足。

卢　娜：那也好。我们是出公差。费用里包括伙食费吗？

琼　斯：是的，只包括早餐和晚餐，既供应中餐又供应西餐。旅客可以根据他们的生活习惯自由选择用餐。

卢　娜：很好。什么饭食？

琼　斯：有米饭、面包、面条等主食。

卢　娜：饮料呢，小姐？

琼　斯：有咖啡、茶、牛奶和矿泉水，想喝什么就喝什么。

卢　娜：我知道啦。餐厅在几楼，小姐？

琼　斯：餐厅在一楼东头。你们既可以在你们的房间用餐也可以到餐厅用餐。

卢　娜：我想这倒不错，挺好的。

第二部

Jones: If you're interested in the rooms, let's go to have a look, shall we?

Luna: OK. I think so. Let's go to have a look.

Jones: Come along with me, please.

Luna: (A few minutes later) Very nice, we'll take them. Please check in.

Jones: Please fill in the traveler's forms first.

Luna: OK. Is that all right?

Jones: Not yet. Might I have your passports?

Luna: Yes. Here you are.

Jones: Here's your key. Please remember when you go out, leave your key at the front desk.

Luna: OK. We can do so.

Jones: Oh. If you need something, just call service girl at the front desk. She can help you to do so.

Luna: Thank you for your warmly reception.

Jones: Serving guests is our general principle.

琼　斯：如果你们对那两个房间感兴趣的话，咱们就先去看看好吗？

卢　娜：好吧。我也是这样想的，咱们就先去看看房间。

琼　斯：请随我来吧。

卢　娜：（几分钟后）很不错，我们就住这儿，请登记吧。

琼　斯：请先填写旅客登记表吧，先生。

卢　娜：好。一切手续都办妥了吗？

琼　斯：还没呢。把你们的护照交给我保管好吗？

卢　娜：好的。给你吧。

琼　斯：这是你们的房间钥匙。请记住你们外出时，把钥匙留给前台保管。

卢　娜：好的，我们会这样做的。

琼　斯：啊，如果你们有什么事要办的话，就给服务台小姐打电话。她会尽力满足你们的要求。

卢　娜：谢谢你热情的接待！

琼　斯：为旅客服务是我们的基本准则。

Formulaic Communication 日常交际习语

Asking Something at a Hotel and Responses 在旅馆询问事情与应答

1. Have you any rooms to be let? 有房间可租吗？

——Please wait a minute. Let me have a check. We have one. 请稍等片刻，我来查一下，有一间。

2. What's the price by day? 按天算，房租是多少？

——Twenty dollars a day. 20 美元一天。

3. Does it include the breakfast and supper? 这里包括不包括使用早餐和晚餐？

——Certainly. It includes. 当然包括。

4. Could I have a single room for two nights please? I didn't book in advance. 我能要个单间住两夜吗？我可没预定。

——Sorry. We're full up. 对不起，人已住满。

5. Perhaps you have a less expensive room. 也许你们有较便宜的房间吧。

6. That's rather more/less than I was expected. 那要比我预期的价钱贵/便宜些。

Explanatory Notes注释：

Come（along）with me/Follow me/This way，please！是祈使句的一种。
祈使句（**Exclamatory Sentence**）表示请求、命令等，动词用原形，句末用
惊叹号"！"或句号"。"，读降调"↘"，在口语中应用得很广泛。例如：

1. 肯定祈使句，**谓语（用动词原形）**。如：

    Be quiet，everybody！　　　　Say it in English！

2. 否定祈使句，**Don't** +**谓语（用动词原形）**。如：

    Don't be afraid！　　　　　　Don't go away！

3. 强调祈使句，**Do** +**谓语（用动词原形）**。如：

    Do come again，please！　　　Do be careful，sir！

4. 强调主语或表明说话对象时，肯定句是 **You** +**谓语（动词原形）**。如：

    You get out of here！你滚出去！

    You clean the concrete mixer and he cleans the mortar mixer！
    你去清理混凝土搅拌机，而他去清理砂浆搅拌机！

5. 强调主语或表明说话对象时，否定句是 **Don't** + **you** +**谓语（动词
    原形）**。如：

    Don't you be late again！你可别再迟到了！

    Don't you make such big noise！你（们）别这样大声吵闹！

6. 强调说话对象是第一人称和第三人称时，第一人称肯定句是 **let me/
    us** +**谓语（动词原形）**；第三人称肯定句是 **Let him/her/them** +**谓语
    （动词原形）**；第一/三人称否定句是 **Let me/us/him/her/them** + **not** +
    谓语（动词原形）。如：

    Let me try once more，sir. 我来再试一次吧，先生。

    Let us/Let's have an English dialogue when we're walking. 散步时，咱
    们进行英语对话吧。

    Let's not waste our time arguing about it. 我们再不要为这事争论不休
    而浪费时间了。

【注】 1. 人们往往都认为 Let us 等于 Let's 或者说 Let's 就是 Let us 的缩
        写形式，其实 Let's 包括对方，而 Let us 并不一定包括对方。

     2. Let + 人称代词的宾格 + not + 谓语（动词原形）是否定句结
        构，在英美人的实际生活中多用 Not + let + 人称代词的宾
        格 + 谓语（动词原形）这种否定句结构。

Spoken Practice口语练习

1. Pair Work：

Imagine that you are Chinese building tenderers who arrive at A London Hotel and want to stay in it for submission of a large project tender. A receptionist asks you how long you are going to stay. You talk with her how to check in a hotel.

2. Tell "true" or "false" in accordance with Learn to Speak English：

1) (　　) They expect to stay more than seven days.

2) (　　) The rooms are nice and beautiful, so the price is too expensive for us to take them.

3) (　　) They came here to travel and should live in a top grade hotel.

4) (　　) Please remember leaving your keys at the front desk when you're out.

5) (　　) Oh. You just phone the service lady at the information desk if you need something.

3. Read & Interpret the following Passage：

Sincerely Advice

Hotel, star hotel and motel rates vary considerable. Before reservation or staying, you'd better to know the price, and then make your decisions. That's a wise action.

4. Give the Four Forms of Following Verbs as the Example Given：

take　　　takes　　　taking　　　took　　　taken

build	stop	study	have	teach	speak	run	use
begin	write	go	help	read	mix	meet	make
put	mean	see	fall	cut	lay	think	tie
be	plan	stand	spell	get	try	pay	do

5. Put the Following Exclamatory Sentences into English or Chinese：

1) 请务必替我向王老板问好!

2) 别怕! 我来帮你!

3) 请跟我来，先生!

4）他有两下子，让他试试吧！

5）危险，可别往楼下扔东西！

6）Be here on time tomorrow! I've some important words to tell you.

7）Do look after yourself! I wish you have a pleasant journey, my old chap.

8）Don't go away! There's a letter for you.

9）Let's not waste our time arguing about it.

10）Talk with foreigners in English if you want to improve your oral English!

6. Substitute the Following Words & Expressions：

1）Use the following **Hotel and Facilities**（饭店/旅馆及其设施）to replace the black words in the following sentence：

Luna：Thank you. Can you have four **single rooms**? Or if you have two **double – bed rooms**, so much the better.

卢　娜：谢谢！能给我们提供四个**单间**吗？如果有两套**双人床房间**，那就更好啦！

Hotel and Facilities ［houˈtel ənd fəˈsilitiz］ 饭店/旅馆及其设施

guesthouse ［ˈgesthaus］ 宾馆

1-5 star hotel ［wʌn tu faiv staːhouˈtel］ 1－5 星级饭店/酒店

Beach Hotel ［biːtʃ houˈtel］ 海滩旅馆

Hot Spring Hotel ［hɔt spriŋ houˈtel］ 温泉旅馆

reception desk/office ［riˈsepʃən desk ˈɔfis］ 总服务台/接待处

information desk ［ˌinfəˈmeiʃən desk］ 问讯处

dining room ［ˈdainiŋ ru(ː)m］ 餐厅

recreation room ［ˌrekriˈeiʃən ru(ː)m］ 游艺厅

bar ［baː］ 酒吧间

Gentlemen's ［ˈdʒentlmenz］ 男盥洗室/男厕

Ladies' ［ˈleidiz］ 女盥洗室/女厕

cloakroom ［ˈklouk ru(ː)m］ 行李寄存处

lobby ［ˈlɔbi］ 大厅

single /double – beded room ［ˈsiŋgl ˈdʌbl bed ru(ː)m］ 单/双人间

three/four-room suite ［θriːfɔː ru(ː)m swiːt］ 三/四套间

health club ［helθ klʌb］ 健身房

night-club ［nait klʌb］夜总会

studio room ［'stju.diou ru(.)m］小型公寓式套间

suite ［swi:t］套间

junior suite ［'dʒu:njə swi:t］单套间

2）Use the following **Information for Filling Forms**（填写表格所用的相关信息）to replace the black words in the following sentence：

Jones：Please fill in **the traveler's forms** first.

琼　斯：请先填写**旅客登记表**吧。

Information for Filling Forms ［ˌinfə'meiʃən fɔ filing fɔ:mz］填写表格所用的相关信息

nationality ［ˌnæʃə'næliti］国籍

given name/last name ［'givn neim la:st neim］名

surname/first name ［'sə:neim fə:st neim］姓

place and date of birth ［pleis ənd deit əv bə:θ］出生地址和出生日期

documents ［'dɔkjumənts］证件

where from ［hwɛə frɔm］从何处来

where to ［hwɛə tu］到何处去

length of stay ［leŋθ əv stei］拟住天数

checking out/in ［'tʃekiŋ aut in］结账离馆/登记进驻

hotel register ［hou'tel 'redʒistə］旅客登记册

booking rooms ［'bukiŋ ru(:)mz］预订房间

room number card ［ru(:)m 'nʌmbə ka:d］房间号码卡

Situational Dialogic Unit 16

第十六情景对话单元

Learn to Speak English

Talking about having Meals in a Restaurant

Carlos：I had my dreakfast rather early this morning. So I'm feeling hungry now.

Brown：Hungry. Now it's ten sharp and earlier to have lunch. Don't you think it would be better to wait a bit and then have a good meal a little bit later?

Carlos：That's OK. But how long shall I wait for you?

Brown：Just an hour. We'll go to have a brunch till we finish our task, right?

Carlos：That's all right. It's a good idea. Let's take the best use of our time then and try to finish it as early as possible.

Brown：What you said is right. Let's work fast.

Carlos：Work with added vigour. It's the first time for me to work on the worksite so I know nothing about it, but wherever and which restaurant shall we go for our brunch?

Brown：Don't worry! There're several restaurants around our worksite. That restaurant where I had last time is quite nice. Let's go there, shall we?

Carlos：That's OK. I'll follow whatever you said if you feel nice, since you're my old brother.

Brown：OK. (an hour later) We've finally accompolished our task.

Carlos：Right. Let's go and take our meal. You go before me and I follow you, OK?

Brown：Oh! OK. Here you are. What do you like to eat? Please order as you like, you'll be my guest today.

Carlos：Thanks a lot. What did you have last time then?

Brown：Fried rice. It's nice and good.

Carlos：We get there, we'll order it, too.

Waiter：Good Morning! Welcome to our restaurant!

Brown：Good Morning!

Waiter：Which would you rather like to have, West food or Chinese food?

学说英语

谈论餐馆就餐

卡洛斯：今天早饭我吃得有点早，所以我现在觉得有点饿。

布　朗：有点饿。现在才 10 点钟，吃午饭还早点儿吧。稍等一会儿，再好好吃一顿，你说好吗？

卡洛斯：那好吧。但得等多长时间？

布　朗：个把小时，等咱们都把手头这点儿活干完后在去吃个早午餐，你说行吗？

卡洛斯：行，行！这倒是个好主意。咱们就抓紧时间吧，争取早点儿完成任务。

布　朗：你说得对，咱们加油干！

卡洛斯：加油干！不过该去哪儿哪家餐馆吃饭为好？我可是首次在这家工地干活，对这儿一无所知。

布　朗：别发愁！工地周边有好几家饭店。上次我吃过那家餐馆就不错。咱们就去那家好吗？

卡洛斯：那好吧，你说可以就成，反正你是老大哥，我听你的。

布　朗：这就好。（一小时后）我们终于完成任务了。

卡洛斯：对呀，咱们这就去吃饭，你前头带路，我紧随其后好吗？

布　朗：啊，好吧。就是这家。你想吃啥？尽管说，今天我请客。

卡洛斯：多谢！你上次吃的什么？

布　朗：炒米饭。味道挺好。

卡洛斯：那我们还要炒米饭吧。

服务员：早上好？欢迎光临本店！

布　朗：早上好？

服务员：请问二位先生想吃什么，西餐还是中餐？

Brown：I'm a Chinese. Naturally I like Chinese food. What do you like to eat then, my young brother?

Carlos：Same as you, old chap. I'd like to have new food as you have though I'm a local person.

Brown：It tells the truth!

Waiter：This is menu. Please order what you like.

Brown：Yeah. Noodles are OK. I haven't had it for a long time.

Carlos：That's all right. I think so.

Waiter：OK. Two bowls of noodles. Would you like something to drink?

Carlos：Bring me a cup of coffee, please. What do you prefer?

Brown：Green tea is nice and good.

Waiter：I see. One moment, please. (Half a minute later) Coffee and tea are ready, please have some. Noodles are about OK.

C. B：Many Thanks! They aren't bad. It really quenches my thirst!

Waiter：Noodles are OK. Please have noodles, and taste whether they're indifferent to fame or gain? Are the noodles very tasty?

Carlos：I think it must be delicious. Please go to help others as you're busy, miss.

Waiter：Thank you for your understanding. You're leisurely and carefree to eat it, Chinese friends.

Carlos：My taste requests more salt. I need just a little salt. Would you be so kind to pass it to me, my old chap?

Brown：All right. But salt in mine is well situated and tast is nice. I feel it is as good as we had it at home.

Carlos：So do I. It is said that the restauranteur is an oversea Chinese.

Brown：Is that so? And how do you know this?

Carlos：Look! Table wares have both knife-fork and chopsticks.

Brown：Yes. No wonder taste is very pure. What would you like to have, Carlos?

Carlos：No, no. Thanks, but I really can't eat any more. Settle accounts, miss.

布　朗：我是中国人，自然喜欢中餐啦。小弟，你可咋办？

卡洛斯：和你一样，老兄。尽管我是当地人，我也想尝个鲜，就随你吧。

布　朗：这倒是句实话。

服务员：这是菜单，请点你们喜欢吃的。

布　朗：好吧。就吃碗面条吧，我好长时间都没吃面条啦。

卡洛斯：好，那也成。

服务员：得！两碗面条。还想喝点什么？

卡洛斯：请给我来杯咖啡。您喝什么？

布　朗：绿茶就挺好。

服务员：我知道了，稍等会儿。（片刻后）咖啡和茶到了，请先喝点儿吧！面条随后就好。

卡　布：多谢！不赖，真解渴！

服务员：面条好了。请用餐，先尝尝咸淡咋样，是否可口？

卡洛斯：我想一定会很可口。小姐，你很忙，先招呼别人去吧。

服务员：中国朋友，谢谢你的理解！尽情吃吧。

卡洛斯：我的口味重，需再加点盐，老兄，把盐递给我好吗？

布　朗：好的。可我的饭咸淡适中，味道不错。我觉得这面条和在国内吃的口感没什么两样。

卡洛斯：我也有同感。听说这家饭店老板是华裔。

布　朗：是吗？你怎么知道的？

卡洛斯：瞧，餐具既有刀叉又有筷子。

布　朗：是呀，难怪味道很地道。还想再吃点啥，卡洛斯？

卡洛斯：不，不用了。谢谢。我实在是吃不下了。结账吧，小姐。

Waiter: Coming. How do you feel? Do you satisfy with the noodles, gentle-men?

Carlos: Yes. I feel it nice, and I've had enough. Thank you for your serving.

Brown: Yes. We all enjoy it very much It's my round, Carlos. It's my treat today. I'll pay.

Carlos: I felt really embarrassed. It makes you spend money!

Brown: I don't think so, as we're brothers and make no distinction between you and me. How much should we pay you, miss?

Waiter: Chinese are hospitable. Ten Dinars is enough. Thank you. Hope you come again!

Brown: The food here is inexpensive but substantial meals, taste is also quite good and Chinese fit for eating here, so we would come again.

Carlos: Yes. We must come to have something if we have chance.

Waiter: Many thanks! Good-bye, sirs.

C. B: Good-bye!

服务员：来啦！感觉怎样？吃得满意吗，二位？

卡洛斯：是的，对啊！感觉不错，也吃得很饱，多谢你的关照。

布　朗：对啊！卡洛斯，这次该我做东。今天我请你，我来付账。

卡洛斯：真不好意思，叫你破费啦！

布　朗：我可不这样认为，因为我们是哥们，不分你我。该付多少钱，小姐？

服务员：中国人就是好客。10 个第纳尔足也。谢谢！希望再次光顾。

布　朗：这儿的饭菜经济实惠，味道可口，适合中国人口味，所以我们还会再来的。

卡洛斯：是的。有机会的话，一定来。

服务员：多谢。诸位先生，走好！

卡　布：再见！

Formulaic Communication 日常交际习语

Asking Meals and Responses 询问就餐与应答

1. What would you like to have? 你想吃些啥？

    ——Anything's all right for me. 我吃什么都行。

2. Would you like some coffee or tea? 你想喝点咖啡还是茶？

    ——I'd like a cup of tea. 我想喝杯茶。

3. May I have just a little to taste? I don't have it in my country.
   给我一点尝尝可以吗？在我国我没吃过这东西。

    ——OK. Make yourself at home. 好啊，请便吧。

4. What kind of special dishes/soup do you have? 你们有什么拿手菜/汤？

    ——Please look at the menu first. 请先看看菜单吧。

5. Help yourself to some fish. 请再吃点儿鱼吧。

    ——Thank you. I'm full/I've had enough. 谢谢。我吃饱了。

    ——No, I enjoy it very much, but I can't have any more. 不要了，我
    很爱吃，但我再也吃不下了。

6. Where shall we go for lunch/dinner? 我们到哪儿去吃午饭/正餐？

    ——Hilton Hotel, I think. 我想希尔顿饭店。

Explanatory Notes注释：

1. Which would you rather have, West food or Chinese food? 请问想吃西餐还是中餐？句中使用的 **would rather** 辅助性动词短语和 **had rather** 可以通用。作假定式的"宁要"解释，表示"将来的选择"讲，比 prefer（宁愿）口气还要委婉。另外句中的 West food or Chinese food 与 which 是同格关系，故为同位语。

2. Would you be so kind to pass it to me? 句中的 **would** 作情态动词用表示现在时态时，这时不论是表达说人本身的意志或向对方提出请求，均比 will 的口气婉转。

3. We'll go to have a **brunch** till we finish our task, right? 句中的 **brunch** 是早饭已过午饭却未到的早中餐，是英语 breakfast 与 lunch 的结合词，也是一种构词法，绝不是个人的发明。这种把两个单词拆开再合成一个新词的方式在当代英语中有进一步发展的趋势，真是屡见不鲜，举不胜举。如：汽车旅馆（motel = motor hotel）、游艇旅馆（botel = boat hotel）、烟雾（smog = smoke fog）等，都是很有创意的构新词法，既拼写简单，记忆容易，又有一目了然的意思。

4. **一般否定式疑问句**的句型是**特殊动词的否定缩写词 + 主语 + 动词 + ?** 这种句子表示请求、看法或惊讶等。如：

   1）**Can't** I pay a visit to your worksite? 我**不能**参观你们工地吗？**No**, you can't. **是的，你不能。**　　　　　**Yes**, you can. **不，你能。**

   2）**Don't** you know the importance to learning English? 你们难道**不知**道学习英语的重要性吗？**Yes**, we do. **不，我们知道。**　　　　**No**, we don't. **是的，我们不知道。**

【注】一般否定疑问句的回答和汉语习惯不同，英语答语的 Yes, No 要和它后面的句子内容一致，而汉语却要以事实一致，所以在回答 Yes 或 No 是一定要慎重使用，在翻译成汉语时一定要把'**Yes**'翻译成汉语的'**不**'；'**No**'翻译成汉语的'**是**'才对。

Spoken Practice 口语练习

1. Pair Work：

A is a Chinese builder. B is a local builder. They're in a working group and work together. A feels a bit hungry by twelve and ask B go to have some food with him. They talk some practical problems, for example, where and what will they go to eat?

2. Answer the Following Questions in accordance with Practical Case：

1）What do you like to eat for your breakfast?

2）Which do you prefer, Chinese food and West food?

3）What do you often have for your lunch?

4）What food do you have to eat if you're a little fat person and on a diet recently?

5）Should you always have very hearty supper?

3. Read & Interpret the Following Passage：

Chinese Restaurants

Asian, especially Chinese travelling to the western countries are often surprised to see a great number of Chinese restaurants—at least one in every city or town. These restaurants offer inexpensive meals or snacks. You order your food and take it to a table yourself. If you order your food 'to go', you take it out of the restaurant.

You must be told here that tipping is not necessary in this kind of restaurant.

4. Learn the Following Words by Heart, Pay Attention to the Changing Forms and Give the Chinese Meaning：

Prefixes-un（dis, non, im, mis, in, ir）= not

1）un	certain	uncertain	happy	unhappy
2）dis	like	dislike ·	agree	disagree
3）non	metal	nonmetal	payment	nonpayment
4）im	material	immaterial	possible	impossible
5）mis	understand	misunderstand	spell	misspell

6) in   convenient   inconvenient   definite   indefinite

7) ir   regular   irregular   removable   irremovable

Suffixes-less /free = not

8) less   hope   hopeless   care   careless

9) free   oil   oil-free   duty   duty-free

5. Put the following English into Chinese：

1) Don't you know the answer to this question? Yes, I do. No, I don't.

2) Isn't the girl over there your classmate?　Yes, she is. No, she isn't.

3) Can't you return to your motherland before finishing project?

    Yes, we can. No, we can't.

4) Doesn't he teach English in the Architectural College?

    Yes, he does. No, he doesn't.

5) Aren't you an inspector in charge of this construction site?

    Yes, I do. No, I don't.

6. Substitute the Following Words & Expressions：

1) Use the following **Restaurant Staff（饭馆职员）** to replace the black words in the following sentence：

Brown：Thanks, but I really can't eat any more. Settle accounts, **waitress**.

布　朗：谢谢，我实在是吃不下了。结账吧，**服务员**。

Restaurant Staff ['restərɔnt staːf] 饭馆职员

Manager ['mænidʒə] 经理

service worker ['səːvis 'wəːkə] 服务员

room attendant [ru(ː)m ə'tendənt] 客房服务员

chamber-maid ['tʃeimbə meid] 客房女服务员

waiter/waitress ['weitə 'weitris] 餐厅男/女服务员

porter ['pɔːtə] 搬运行李服务员

guest [gest] 旅客，宾客

2) Use the following **Chinese Staple /Principal Food（中餐主食）** to replace the black words in the following sentence：

Waiter：Which would you rather have, **West food** or **Chinese food**?

服务员：请问想吃**西餐**还是**中餐**?

Brown：We're Chinese. Naturally we all like **Chinese food.**

布　　朗：我们是中国人，自然喜欢**中餐**啦。

Chinese Staple ／Principal Food ［ˈtʃainiz steipl prinsəpəl fuːd ］

中餐主食

noodles with oil ［ˈnuːdlz wið oil］油泼面（条）

noodles with soup ［ˈnuːdlz wið sup ］汤面（条）

fried noodles ［fraid ˈnuːdlz ］炒面（条）

rice-flour noodles ［rais ˈflauə ˈnuːdlz ］米粉

（cooked）rice ［ kukt rais ］米饭

fried rice ［ fraid rais ］炒米饭

rice gruel；porridge ［rais gruəl ˈpɔridʒ］稀饭；粥

millet gruel ［ˈmilit gruəl］小米稀饭

maize gruel ［meiz gruəl ］豆米粥

soybean = soya milk ［ˈsɔibiːn ˈsɔiə milk ］豆浆

steamed bun／bread ［ˈstiːmd bʌn bred ］馒头

steamed twisted roll ［ˈstiːmd ˈtwistid rɔl ］花卷

silver-thread roll ［ˈsilvə θred rɔl ］银丝卷

steamed sponge cake ［ˈstiːmd spɔŋ keik ］蜂糕

multi-layer steamed bread ［ˈmʌlti-leiə ˈstiːmd bred ］千层饼

thin pancake ［θin ˈpænkeik］荷叶饼

fried shredded pancake ［fraid ˈʃredid ˈpænkeik ］炒饼

lightly fried dumpling ［ˈlaitli fraid ˈdʌmpliŋ］锅贴

deep-fried twisted dough sticks ［ˈdiːp fraid ˈtwistid dou stiks ］油饼

pyramid-shaped dumpling made of glutinous rice wrapped in

［ˈpirəmid ʃeipd ˈdʌmpliŋ meid əv ˈgluːtinəs rais ˈræpd in ］粽子

sweet dumpling made of glutinous rice flour（for the Lantern Festival）

［ swiːt ˈdʌmpliŋ meid əv ˈgluːtinəs rais ˈflauə fə ðə ˈlæntən ˈfestəvəl］元宵

【注】这一会话单元仅提供了部分中餐主食，肯定不能满足实际的需要。假如需要中西餐的其他主食、盘菜以及酒、饮料等，可查看《建筑技术与管理英语情景会话》第十一情景会话单元 谈论祝贺与宴请 参阅第76－78页。

Situational Dialogic Unit **17**

第十七情景对话单元

Learn to Speak English

Talking about Vacation Sight-seeing

Benson: It's weekend today. I want to go around.

Carroll: You should wander, I think. You travelled far away across the sea, and went to the trouble of traveling a long distance and finally come to my motherland to help us construct. It's a good idea that you'll go sight-seeing in your holidays!

Benson: Thank you for your understanding. We've just been to your country, and know nothing about here. Would you please tell me what attractive places here to be seen?

Carroll: You left your native hometown, and it's a far away from the East. By comparation with my country, naturally there's a great difference between the two countries, right?

Benson: Right. So the local conditions and customs, interesting places and famous mountains and great rivers here are all worth sight-seeing.

Carroll: What you thought is right.

Benson: You could explain the profound in simply terms and the comparative approach you adopted is heartfelt wishes the aspiration of us. So it might say that only you know me.

Carroll: You flatter me. Let's make a long story short, what would you like to see, places of historic interest or famous montains and great rivers, I worder?

Benson: To put it bluntly, I like all. And what interesting places are there in and around our city, I'd like to know?

Carroll: Yes, of course. Your meaning goes sight-seeing from our side first.

Benson: What you said is absolutely right. We couldn't seek far and wide for what lies close at hand, right?

Carroll: Right, it's the reason, too. The city where we're living is an ancient one.

学说英语

谈论假日观光旅游

本　森：今天是周末，我想出去逛逛。

卡罗尔：我想你应该逛逛。你漂洋过海，不远万里来到我国帮助我们搞建设！利用节假日出去观光倒是一个好主意呀！

本　森：感谢你的理解。可我们初到贵国，对这儿旅游景点一无所知。请告诉我贵国有哪些好玩的地方？

卡罗尔：你们背井离乡，来自遥远的东方，和贵国相比这里自然有许多不同之处对吗？

本　森：对啊。所以这儿的风土人情、名胜古迹、名山大川都值得一看。

卡罗尔：你这样认为就对了。

本　森：你能这样深入浅出的解释，用对比的方法说出了我的心声，可以这样说，知我者，莫过于你也。

卡罗尔：过奖过奖。咱们还是长话短说吧，不知你喜欢观光名胜古迹还是游览名山大川？

本　森：说句不客气话，都喜欢。我想知道我们所在的城市周边有哪些可看的地方吗？

卡罗尔：当然有。你的意思先是从我们身边看起。

本　森：就是这个意思，我们不能舍近求远，你说对吗？

卡罗尔：对，也是这个理。我们所居住的就是一座具有悠久历史的古城。

Benson: Yes, I think there might be many historic interets to be viewed and admired here,

Carroll: Yes, indeed. You're builders, undoubtly the buildings are first for you to pay a visit.

Benson: Certainly. We may learn and introduce your advance construction skills through visiting.

Carroll: So we pay a visit to the Imperial Palace first. There're many buildings there to be seen.

Benson: This is a good idea for killing two birds with one stone. Is it far away from here? Then we've to go there by bus, OK?

Carroll: OK, by bus. Actually it's not so far. I think half an hour is enough for us to go there by bus.

Benson: It's a good idea that go by bus at once.

Carroll: (half an hour later) Here you are. Our country is an island country, you must know. The Imperial Palace was surely built on the highest place.

Benson: Yes, it's the same concept to build the palace of emperor in our country, that symbol of king's position and right is supreme.

Carroll: Is it so? I've never thought such thing.

Benson: Absolutely right, I surppose all the kings in the world must think so. The kings in yours aren't exception, either.

Carroll: Your knowledge is broad and profound and even catches King's mind.

Benson: It's an ordinary psychological activity. You're a local person and know here like back of your hand, so you'll go ahead, I'll trail along behind you.

Carroll: Sound reasonable. To be frank with you, I've been here many times. I'm not sure that I can become an amateur tourist guide.

Benson: You're sure to become one and this is unquestionable, and together with your cleverness, you mustn't make me disappoint.

Carroll: Thank you for your trust. Let's go through the Golden Gate Bridge first.

本　森：的确如此。我想这儿一定有许多名胜古迹有必要观赏。

卡罗尔：的确如此。你们是建设者，毫无疑问建筑物是你们首选的参观项目。

本　森：当然是。因为通过参观，我们可以学习和借鉴你们优秀的建造技术。

卡罗尔：那就先参观王宫，那儿有很多建筑物可供参观。

本　森：这才是个一举两得的好主意！离这儿远吗？得乘车是吗？

卡罗尔：是的，得乘车。其实并不远。我想乘半小时车足矣。

本　森：我们马上就去乘车，这是个好主意。

卡罗尔：（半小时后）就是这儿。你一定知道我国是一个岛屿之国，国王宫肯定也就建在最高处。

本　森：对，这和我国皇宫的建造理念完全一样，象征着其地位和权力的至高无上。

卡罗尔：是吗？可我从未想过这事。

本　森：绝对没错。我认为世界上国王肯定都是这样的心态，你们的国王也不例外。

卡罗尔：你的知识渊博，就连国王的心思都知道。

本　森：这是人的正常心理活动。你是本地人，肯定来过这儿，对这儿了如指掌，你前头领路，我步你后尘。

卡罗尔：言之有理。不瞒你说，这儿我来过多次，没准，我能成为一名业余导游。

本　森：你肯定会成为的，这是无可置疑的。再加上你的机灵劲儿，你一定不会令我失望的。

卡罗尔：谢谢你的信任。咱们就先过金门桥吧。

Benson: OK. I suppose that the bridge likes the Golden Water Bridge between Tian An Men (Gate of Heavenly Peace) and Square in our capital plays a role of linking two places, and both were built in unique style.

Carroll: I think so. Look! The clear and blue water under the bridge gives people enjoyable feeling.

Benson: All right. Sight – seeing is to look for it.

Carroll: Oh, yes. How about lily pond?

Benson: It's simply wonderful! The fountain in the middle of the lily pond is so beautiful that one simply can't take them all in, too wonderful for words. I'm really fascinating and overwhelmed by them.

Carroll: Right. They're only man-made wonders, and there's also a natural scenic spot for you to enjoy.

Benson: What natural scenic spot is it? Quickly show me to sight-see it, OK?

Carroll: OK. Please raise your head and look.

Benson: Oh, the waterfall on the mountains is really magnificent and also seldom to see. And it's too beautiful for words.

Carroll: Certainly. These're churches and Buddhist temples. What do you think about architecture?

Benson: Not bad. I know their intention usage by outlooking.

Carroll: Look! Stone forests are on the left and old pagodas on the right.

Benson: They're rationally distrbuted. It's the beautiful and old Imperial Palace, isn't?

Carroll: Yeah. You've a good eyesight and be worthy of builder travelled widely.

Benson: It's nothing. Some types of the buildings here are same as ours. Especially European types, out of ordernary and afford much food for thought.

Carroll: All right. You must know that our motherland was a colony for the British Empire, so British typicality is incisively and vividly.

Benson: No matter who have built them, we should modestly learn from them in order to play up strengths and avoid weakness and improve our construction quality. Bring benefit to mankind.

本　森：好。我想这金门桥的作用和我国首都的天安门与广场之间的金水桥很相似，起着连接两地的作用，而且建造得都很别致。

卡罗尔：我想也是。看！桥下这清澈蔚蓝的水给人一种温馨的感觉。

本　森：对，游览就是要这种感觉。

卡罗尔：啊！是。再看这荷花池修建得咋样？

本　森：简直好极啦！荷花池再加上中央这喷泉真是美不胜收，妙在不言中，的确迷人，令人折服。

卡罗尔：对。这只是人造奇观，还有自然景观等着你欣赏。

本　森：什么自然景观，快领去看看好吗？

卡罗尔：好。你抬头看。

本　森：啊，山上的瀑布确实壮观，也十分罕见。这太美了，美得无法形容。

卡罗尔：当然是。这些是教堂与佛寺，你觉得建造的怎样？

本　森：不错，从外观一看就知道设计者的意图。

卡罗尔：看！左边是石林，而右边是古塔。

本　森：布局合理。这就是美丽而又古老的国王宫殿吧？

卡罗尔：是啊，你很有眼力，真不愧是走南闯北的建设者。

本　森：哪里哪里！这里建筑物和我国的有类同之处，但更具有欧洲风格，与众不同，耐人寻味。

卡罗尔：对。我国曾是英帝国的殖民地，所以英国建筑特点体现得淋漓尽致，随处可见。

本　森：不管是谁建造的，我们都应该虚心学习人家之长补己之短，以提高我们的施工质量，造福于民。

Carroll: What you said is very fine. This is an aim for every builder to forever seek. What do you think today? Do you have a good time?

Benson: Yes, very happy. It's a worthwhile trip, my worth while to see indeed and really enjoy myself so much as to forget to go home.

Carroll: Isn't it? So I'm relieved. It's well said that you can't say you've been to our country until you've see the Imperial Palace.

Benson: Such words are from the bottom of my heart. If there's a chance, you'd better accompany me and go sight-seeing the scenic spots, and famous mountains and great rivers in your country, OK?

Carroll: No problem at all. If you're interesting and I've time, I must go with you.

Benson: I really don't know how to thank you enough.

Carroll: As apprentice does what he could do for his master, so ther're no need to mention it at all, otherwise I'll feel I'm being treated as a stranger.

Benson: That's it. But your behavior is worthy of praise. Let's help each other.

卡罗尔：你说得可真好！这是我们每一位建设者永远追求的目标。你
　　　　觉得今天玩得怎样？开心吗？

本　森：是的，高兴，不虚此行，确实值得一看，真叫人流连忘返。

卡罗尔：可不是吗？这么说我就放心了。常言说得好啊，没有游览过
　　　　王宫不能说你到过贵国。

本　森：我可是肺腑之言。有机会还能陪我再观光贵国风景，看看名
　　　　山大川吗？

卡罗尔：没问题，只要你有兴趣，我有时间，一定奉陪。

本　森：我真不知该怎样感谢你为好。

卡罗尔：徒弟给师傅做点事没必要这么客气，否则不就见外了吗？

本　森：这就对了。但你的行为值得称赞。咱们应该互相帮助。

Formulaic Communication 日常交际习语

Asking the Sight-seeing and Responses 询问观光与应答

1. Is there anything interesting to see here? 这儿有什么有趣的东西可看吗?

    ——Yes, of course. Let's make a day of it. 当然有。咱们痛痛快快地玩一天吧。

2. Are there any places of historical remains in your country? 贵国有什么历史遗迹吗?

    ——Yes, there're. 是的，有。

3. What's this city famous for? 这座城市以什么而著名?

    ——The city/here is famous for ancient architecture. 这个城市/这儿以古建而闻名于世。

4. Where's your favorite haunt? 你最爱去什么地方?

    ——My favorite haunt is the Great Wall of China. 我最爱去的地方是中国的长城。

5. What's the most important feature about this city? 这个城市有什么主要特色?

    ——Tourism. 旅游业。

6. How did you spend your last weekend? 你上个周末是怎样度过的?

    ——(We spent our last weekend in) Travalling by car/ship/plane. (我们上周) 乘汽车/船/飞机旅行度过的。

7. What's your plan for this weekend/summer vacation? 你计划这个周末/暑假做什么?

    ——My plan is to make a round-the-world tour. 我的计划是做一次环球旅行。

8. Let's make a day of it. 咱们痛痛快快的玩一天。

9. I'd like to buy some souvenirs. 我想买些纪念品。

Explanatory Notes注释:

1. 句中的 go sight-seeing（去观光）是 **go + doing** 句型（**去做某事**）。这是个很有用的句型，又如：go mountain-climbing 去爬山，go shopping 去购物，go fishing 去钓鱼，go swimming 去游泳，go hunting 去打猎，go camping 去野营等。

2. go to school（上学）是 **go to + n. 句型**，与上句注释完全不同，其中 **go to 的 to 为介词，由于 to 是介词，所以 to 后只能用名词**。如：go to work 上班，go to hospital 去医院，go to church 去做礼拜，go to town/city 去进城，go to worksite 去工地。

3. go to see = go and see（去看看）。这里有两点值得注意：

    1）go to see 中的 to 不同与上句中的 to，这里的 **to 是不定式符号表示目的**。

    2）由于 go to see 这里的 to 是不定式符号，所以其后只能跟动词原形。

4. 感叹句的特殊形式：

    1）在陈述句，祈使句，和疑问句后加感叹号变成感叹句以表示强烈的感情。如：

    Do work with us!　　　　　（祈使句）一定要和我们在一起工作！

    She speaks English so fluently!（陈述句）他英语讲得多么流利呀！

    Have you read such a moving book!（疑问句）你看过这么动人的书！

    2）用一个词或词组表示强烈的感情也是一种感叹句。如：

    Well done/said/spoken/written!　做/说/讲/写得好！

    Wonderful! 好极了!　　　　　　　A good idea! 好主意!

    3）以 there, here 等副词开头的感叹句。如果代词作主语时，there, here 等副词置于动词之前；如果名词作主语时，there, here 等副词却置于动词之后。如：

    Here it comes!（车）来了! →Here comes Green!　　格林来了!

    There she is! 她在哪儿! 　→There goes the bell!　　铃声响了!

    Off they went! 他们走了! →Up and away flew the bird! 鸟飞走了!

Spoken Practice 口语练习

1. Pair Work:

Imagine that you're Chinese builders who come to construct in a large city abroad. Team leader asks you to make a sight-seeing schedule for your weekend and some holidays. What do you do before or after making the sight-seeing schedule? Please talk with your workmen about this topical sight-seeing schedule.

2. Answer the Following Questions in accordance with Practical Case:

1) Where is your favorite haunt in this country?

2) What's the most important feature about this city?

3) Let's make a sight-seeing schedule this spring festival, shall we?

4) Is there anything interesting place to see in your city?

5) What's this city famous for, I'd love to know?

3. Read & Interpret the Following Passage:

The World Tourist Resort ——Xi'an

Xi'an, called Chang'an in history, is Chinese cultural source and cultural representative, condenses 5000 years Chinese civilization of the genetic gene, Tang Chang'an City was China's first international metropolis, Xi'an internationalization characteristics is with Chinese temperamental culture. It served intermitterly as the capital of Zhou、Qin、Han、Sui、Tang and others, totally thirteen dynasties and spanning more than 1100 years a long history, it's the most important place which founded capitals and built dynasties in China, the oldest capital of the longest time which built dynasties, and it's one of the four ancient capitals in the world too. Beginning in the Han Dynasty, Xi'an was already an important city for international exchange between China and many countries and it was also the very starting point of the wellknown "Silk Road", which promotes Han and post-Han international economic and cultural exchange. Xi'an with its cultural heritage and artistic treasure-house are known to the world, so Xi'an is a world city and culture capital that has already become one of the world's most famous tourist scenic spot. As the saying that you can't say you've been to China until you've sightseen Xi'an. Therefore every year more than millions of visitors come and sight-see in Xi'an.

4. **Change the following into Exclamatory Sentences as Examples given:**

   A. **Xiao Hua speaks English very fluently.**

   →**How fluently Xiao Hua speaks English**!

   1) It's wonderful to sightsee in London City with you.

   →**How** _____!

   2) Chinese builders work very hard.

   →**How** _____!

   3) I want to see you once more.

   →**How** _____!

   4) The rain fell.

   →**How** _____!

   5) The weather is lovely here.

   →**How** _____!

   B. **Xi'an is an ancient and beautiful city.**

   →**What an ancient and beautiful city Xi'an is**!

   6) He and I are kind friends.

   →**What** _____!

   7) It's an interesting and moving story Mr. Ma told us last class.

   →**What** _____!

   8) They're setting up a large and high building now.

   →**What** _____!

   9) It's a lovely place in Africa.

   →**What** _____!

   10) She's made great progress in her English studies.

   →**What** _____!

5. **Put the following Exclamatory Sentences into English or Chinese:**

   1) 好主意! _____

2）这些学生多用功呀！＿＿＿＿＿＿＿＿＿＿＿＿＿＿

3）飞机飞走了！＿＿＿＿＿＿＿＿＿＿＿＿＿＿＿＿＿＿＿

4）天气多么好呀！＿＿＿＿＿＿＿＿＿＿＿＿＿＿＿＿＿

5）Wonderful！＿＿＿＿＿＿＿＿＿＿＿＿＿＿＿＿＿＿＿＿

6）She speaks English so fluently！＿＿＿＿＿＿＿＿＿

7）What a pity！＿＿＿＿＿＿＿＿＿＿＿＿＿＿＿＿＿＿＿

8）How hard they work！＿＿＿＿＿＿＿＿＿＿＿＿＿＿

9）How I want to see you！＿＿＿＿＿＿＿＿＿＿＿＿＿

10）How time flies！＿＿＿＿＿＿＿＿＿＿＿＿＿＿＿＿＿

6. Substitute the Following Words & Expressions：

1）Use the following **Terms about Sight-seeing Landscapes**（观光/旅游景观）to replace the black words in the following sentence：

Benson：Oh, **the waterfall on the mountains** is really magnificent and also seldom to see.

本　森：啊，山上的瀑布确实壮观，也十分罕见。

Terms about Sight-seeing Landscapes ［ tɔːmz əˈbaut ˈsaitˌsiːiŋ ˈlændzkeips］观光/旅游景观

places of historical interest［ˈpleisiz əv hisˈtɔrikəl ˈintrist］历史名胜

places of interest［ˈpleisiz əv ˈintrist］古迹

historical site［hisˈtɔrikəl sait］历史遗迹

historical relics［hisˈtɔrikəl ˈreliks］历史文物

beautiful old ruins［ˈbjuːtəful ould ˈru(ː)inz］美丽而又古老的废墟

historic museum［hisˈtɔrik ˈmju(ː)ziəm］历史博物馆

scenic spot［ˈsiːnik spɔt］风景区

natural wonders［ˈnætʃərəl ˈwʌndəz］自然奇景

man-made wonder［mæn-meid ˈwʌndə］人造奇观

famous mountains and great rivers［ˈfeiməs ˈmauntinz ənd griːt ˈrivəz］名山大川

the sights of the country/ city［ðə saits əv ðə ˈkʌntri /ˈsiti］农村/城市风光

landscape［ˈlændzkeip］风景

views［vju：z］景色

unearthed cultural relics［'ʌn'ə：θid 'kʌltʃərəl 'reliks］出土文物

the ruins of Rome/Roma［ðə 'ru：inz əv roum］古罗马遗址

well-known place［well noun pleis］名胜

scenic wonder［'si：nik 'wʌndəz］风景胜地

seven wonders of the world［'sevn 'wʌndəz əv ðə wə：ld］（古代）世界七大奇迹

mountain city［'mauntin 'siti］山城

mountain villa［'mauntin 'vilə］山庄

mountain area［'mauntin 'ɛəriə］山区

mountain spring［'mauntin spriŋ］山泉

cultural objects［'kʌl tʃərəl 'ɔbdʒekts］文物

curios［'kjuəriəuz］古玩，古董

antiquities［æn'tikwitiz］古物，古迹

natural scenery［'nætʃərəl 'si：nəri］自然风景

attractive scenery［ə'træktiv 'si：nəri］动人风景

great hill and clear waters［gri：t hil ənd kliə 'wɔ：təz］山明水秀

picturesque scenery［ˌpiktʃə'resk 'si：nəri］山清水秀

picturesque architecture［ˌpiktʃə'resk 'a：kitetʃə］别致的建筑

picturesque mountain city/village［ˌpiktʃə'resk 'mauntin 'siti 'vllidʒ］景色如画的山城/村庄

2）Use the following **Terms about Sight-seeing**（游览/观光术语）to replace the black words in the following sentence：

Carroll：Sound reasonable. To be frank with you, I've been here many times. I'm not sure that I can become an amateur **tourist guide.**

卡罗尔：言之有理。不瞒你说，这儿我来过多次，没准，我能成为一名业余**导游**。

Terms about Sight-seeing［tə：mz ə'baut 'saitˌsi：iŋ］游览/观光术语

sight-seeing party［'saitˌsi：iŋ 'pa：ti］游览/观光团

sight-seer［'saitˌsi：ə］游客，观光者

sight-seeing schedule［'saitˌsi：iŋ 'ʃedju：l］游览/观光计划

a copy of sight-seeing itinerary [ə ˈkɔpi əv ˈsaitˌsiːiŋ aiˈtinərəri] 游览／观光计划表

sight-seeing route [ˈsaitˌsiːiŋ ruːt] 游览／观光路线

have a boat ride on the lake [hæv ə bout raid ɔn ðə leik] 坐船在湖上游玩

take some pictures of buildings [teik sʌm vjuz əv ˈbildiŋ] 拍几张建筑照片

Situational Dialogic Unit **18**

第十八情景对话单元

Learn to Speak English

Talking about Weather

Bart: We're going to make roofing waterproof works tomorrow, and I forgot to listen to the weather report. Did you listen to it, Carl?

Carl: Yes, I did it just now.

Bart: Can you tell me what the Weather Forecast said?

Carl: Yes, of course. It's going to rain tomorrow.

Bart: Don't crack a joke. I don't believe it at all. What fine weather it is! But it's nice and bright now, it's a beautiful day, you see. How is it going to rain tomorrow?

Carl: As the saying goes: A storm may arise from a clear sky; something unexpected may happen any time that modifying weather changes is not normal. Changing weather is normal.

Bart: Apparently, it's going to be sunny day and also to be cloudy day.

Carl: Bless from heaven! I hope it keeps fine till this weekend.

Bart: I wish it were true. Because New World Mansion is under construction, otherwise construction period will be postponed. The works won't be completed on time.

Carl: I understand your thought and worry about changing weather can hold up normal construction. What's the temperature today, sir?

Bart: It has climbed to 25 degrees above zero.

Carl: It's neither cold nor hot, moderate temperature. It's the best time for us to construct.

Bart: Speak in a rational and convincing way.

Carl: All right. I suggest you give up your weekend and make the roofs of water proof so as to be completion of the works ahead of schedule.

Bart: That's a good idea. I'm sure that I'll adopt yours.

学说英语

谈论气候

巴　特：我们明天要做屋面防水工程，可我却忘了听天气预报，你听了吗，卡尔？

卡　尔：是的，我刚听过。

巴　特：能告诉我是怎么预报的吗？

卡　尔：当然能。明天有雨。

巴　特：别开玩笑！我根本不信。（天气）多么好呀！你看现在还是阳光明媚，天气宜人。明天（天气）怎么会下雨呢？

卡　尔：常言道：天有不测风云就是形容天气的变化是无常的，说变就变是很正常的。

巴　特：显然（天气）会转晴也会变阴。

卡　尔：老天保佑！但愿（天气）能如人愿，到周末都是好天气。

巴　特：但愿如此。因为新世界大厦正在施工中。否则工期就得推迟，工程就不能如期竣工。

卡　尔：我理解你的心情，担心天气变化会影响正常的施工，先生。今天的气温怎样？

巴　特：气温已上升到25℃。

卡　尔：天气不冷不热，温度适中，正是施工的好时光。

巴　特：言之有理。

卡　尔：对，我建议你们放弃周末休息时间做屋面防水，确保提前完成工程进度。

巴　特：这倒是个好主意。我一定采纳你的建议。

Formulaic Communication 日常交际习语

Asking the Weather and Responses 询问天气与应答

1. How's the weather in Xi'an yesterday? 昨天西安天气怎样？

   ——The weather/ It was fine in Xi'an yesterday，neither hot nor cold，It's bright sunshine and gentle breeze. 昨天西安天气很不错，不热不冷，真是风和日暖。

2. What's the weather like today? 今天天气怎样？

   ——It's getting cold today. 今天在变冷。

3. What's the temperature today? 今天气温是多少？

   ——（It's ）Twenty above zero. 零上20℃。

4. Does it often rain here in April? 春季这儿常下雨吗？

   ——No, it doesn't. 不，不常下。

5. Is it always as hot as in summer? 夏季总是这样热吗？

   ——Yes, sometimes. 是的，有时是。

6. What a lovely day! 多么好的天气！

Explanatory Notes 注释：

1. **What fine weather it is**！（天气多么好呀！）

   这是个感叹句（**imperative sentence**）。感叹句在英语口语会话中经常使用，因此一定要掌握好。掌握好该句，首先要知道感叹句表示喜愁哀乐等强烈感情，句末一律用惊叹号"！"，读降调"↘"；其次要知道构成英语感叹句常使用 What/How（多么）这两个词，但这两个词怎么用，也就是在什么情况用 What，在什么情况用 How 是一个实质性的问题，很有必要给予解释以利于今后科学运用的根据。要掌握好感叹句必须注意下列三点：

   1）感叹句的句型：**How/What + 所修饰的词（+主语+谓语）+！** （这里的主语＋谓语是陈述句的语序，为简练起见也可以省略。）

   2）**What** 的用法：

   What 是形容词，只能作定语修饰名词，但该名词前也可用形容词作定语或冠词来限定，其句型应是 **What +（a/形容词+）名词（+主语+谓语）+！** 例如：

   What hardworking **students** they are! 他们是多用功的学生呀！

   What a beautiful **house** this is! 这是一栋多么漂亮的房子呀！

   What a **pity**（it is）! 多么可惜呀！

   3）**How** 的用法：

   How 是副词在句中作状语，修饰形容词、副词或动词，其句型应是 **How +形容词/副词/动词 +（主语+谓语）+！** 例如：

   How **tired** he is! 他多么累呀！（How 修饰形容词）

   How **hard** they work! 他们工作得多么努力呀！（How 修饰副词）、

   How **lovely** the weather is! 天气多么好呀！（How 修饰副词）

   How I **want** to see you! 我多么想看见你呀！（How 修饰动词）

2. I wish it were true = Let's hope so. 但愿如此。

Spoken Practice 口语练习

1. Pair Work：

Work in groups or pairs. Suppose you're an engineering inspector. Ask your partner to give you a brief introduction about weather recently in order to accomplish your construction task and complete the project by scheduled time.

2. Answer the Following Questions in accordance with Practical Case：

1）What's the weather today?

2）How's the weather in your hometown the day before yesterday?

3）Do you often listen to the weather forecast? Is it going to rain?

4）What's the temperature those days?

5）Do you like the weather in Bejing?

3. Read & Interpret the Following Passage：

The Weather

A very common way to start a conversation is to talk about the weather in the Western countries, especially in Britain. This point is totally different from ours. The reason for this is not simply that the weather is interesting and variable, but that the British are reluctant to converse about personal matters with others who are not kith and kin. Mentioning the weather can be a useful and inoffensive way of starting a conversation with a stranger anywhere. Chinese should know the way in order that we'd better to communicate with them.

4. Change the following into Exclamatory Sentences as Examples given：

A. How clean and tidy your building site is!

→What a clean and tidy building site it is!

1）How long Changjiang（the Yantse River）is!

　　→What _____!

2）How quiet the places are!

　　→What _____!

3）How hard they're working!

　　→What _____!

4）How fast and well those builders have done！

→What _____！

5）How comfortable this sitting room is！

→What _____！

B. **What high and beautiful buildings Chinese constructors set up！**

→**How high and beautiful Chinese constructors set up the buildings！**

6）What a sweet voice Marry songs！

→How _____！

7）What heavy tower crane hoisters are erecting！

→How _____！

8）What a good drawing they're designing！

→How _____！

9）What a pretty girl and handsame boy they are！

→How _____！

10）What difficult task he accomplished！

→How _____！

5. Fill in the Blankets with What or How according to Grammatical Rule：

1）_____ happy！

2）_____ the rain fell！

3）_____ beautiful buildings they are building！

4）_____ a funny story our teacher told us last class！

5）_____ clean and tidy your construction site is！

6）_____ heavy tools the stone cuter are taking with him！

7）_____ I wonder what you are！

8）_____ an idea！

9）_____ a sweet voice the girl has！

10）_____great progress our classmates have made in their English studies！

6. Substitute the Following Words & Expressions：

1）Use the following **Terms about Weather（天气相关用语）** to re-place the black words in the following sentence：

Bart：What did the Weather Forecast say？

巴　特：怎么预报的？

Carl：It's going to **rain** tomorrow.

卡　尔：明天要下雨。

Terms about Weather ［tə:mz ə'baut 'weðə］天气相关用语

weather forecast ［'weðə 'fɔ:ka:st］天气预报

fine/sunny day ［fain 'sʌni dei］晴天

cloudy day ［'klaudi dei］阴天

rainy/dry day ［rein drai dei］雨/干旱天

snowy/windy day ［snoui windi dei］雪/风天

white frost ［hwait frɔst］白霜

dense fog ［dens fɔg］大雾

cold/hot/warm day ［kould hɔt wɔ:m dei］冷/热/暖天

afterglow ［a:'ftəglou］晚霞

rainbow ［'reinbou］彩虹

mild/vile climate ［maild vail 'klaimeit］温和/恶劣气候

fine/fair weather ［fain fɛə 'weðə］好天气

bad/ foul weather ［bæd faul 'weðə］坏天气

humidity ［'hju(:)miditi］湿度/气

temperature ［'tempəreitʃə］温度

precipitation ［ˌpresipi'teiʃən］雨量

wind force ［'wind fɔ:s］风力

2）Use the following **Terms about temperature**（气温相关用语）to replace the black words in the following sentence：

Carl：... What's the **temperature** today, sir?

卡　尔：……今天的**气温**怎样. 先生?

Bart：It has climbed to 20 **degrees above** zero.

巴　特：气温已上升到**20**℃。

at... degree below zero ［ət... di'gri: bi'lou 'ziərou］在零下……度

at... degree above zero ［ət... di'gri: ə'bʌv 'ziərou］在零上……度

Centigrade themometer ［'sentigreid θə'mɔmitə］摄氏温度计

Fahrenheit themometer ［'færənhait θə'mɔmitə］华氏温度计

minimum temperature ［'miniməm 'tempəritʃə］最低温度

maximum temperature ［'mæksiməm 'tempəritʃə］最高温度

Situational Dialogic Unit 19

第十九情景对话单元

Learn to Speak English

Talking about Date

Jack: Hello! When did you arrive in my country, Chinese friend?

Limi: At noon, the day before yesterday, sir.

Jack: You're all here now. What time are you going to start the ground breaking for the International Airport, I'd love to know?

Limi: According to the construction contract, next spring, that's to say, on January 3rd, 2006 after new year's holidays.

Jack: But what's the date today?

Limi: Today is December 30th, 2005.

Jack: How time flies! In an instant, it's time for starting the construction. And what day is today?

Limi: Sorry. I'm too busy to care about it. Let me check the calendar. Oh, today is Wednesday.

Jack: How many days are there to be left, sir?

Limi: Let me consider and then say. There're only four days for us to start the ground breaking. We can normally start it if there're not any special conditions.

Jack: I think so.

Limi: In order to be started on schedule, all the workers and staff haven't any rest for several weeks and be awfully busy. Maybe you don't know we're tired with aching back and legs.

Jack: How hard you work! Work is important but health is more important, do you think it's all right?

学说英语

谈论日期

杰　克：喂！中国朋友，您何时抵达我们国家的？

李　眠：前天中午抵达贵国的，先生。

杰　克：现在你们都来了。我想知道你们何时破土动工国际机场工程？

李　眠：依照施工合同规定的日期，应是明年春季，也就是2006年元月3日。

杰　克：那今天几号啦？

李　眠：今天是2005年12月30日。

杰　克：时间过得可真快呀！转眼开工时间就到了。今天是星期几？

李　眠：对不起，我忙得还没顾上这事，我得查一下日历。啊，今天是星期三。

杰　克：距离破土动工还有几天时间，先生？

李　眠：让我算算再说，仅剩下四天时间。特殊情况除外，我们会正常动工的。

杰　克：我想也是。

李　眠：为了确保如期开工，广大职工好几周都没休息，忙得不亦乐乎，也许你并不知道把我们都累得腰酸背痛。

杰　克：辛苦了！工作重要，但身体更重要，你说对吗？

Limi: All right, it goes without saying. But it further proves Chinese are the men of standing to their word, and they never make a promise they can not keep. Thank you for your reminding and concern.

Jack: Don't mention it. You must combine working with rest. Now how about your preparation?

Limi: I don't keep secret. All is ready except what is crucial.

Jack: I was worried about you until you told me this. Hope you win victory in the first battle and win success immediatelly upon arrival.

Limi: Thank you for your lucky words.

李　眯：对。这是不言而喻的。但要进一步证明中国人是说一不二的，他们答应的事一定能够办到。谢谢你的提醒和关心。

杰　克：甭客气。你们一定得劳逸结合。那现在准备到什么程度了？

李　眯：不瞒你说，万事俱备，只欠东风。

杰　克：我这就放心啦。祝你们旗开得胜，马到成功！

李　眯：多谢你的吉言。

Formulaic Communication 日常交际习语

Asking Date and Responses 询问日期与应答

1. What day (of the week) is (it) today? 今天是星期几?

——Today /It's... 今天是……。

2. What's the date today? 今天几号了?

——Today is/It's ... 今天是……

3. What month will the Labour Competition take place? 劳动竞赛在哪个月举行?

——In February. 在二月。

4. What season do you like best? 你最喜欢哪个季节?

——Of course, spring. 当然是春季。

5. Which year/When were you born? 你哪年出生的?

—— I was born in... 我出生于……

6. When is Christmas/Thanksgiving? 圣诞节/感恩节是何时?

——Christmas Day is the twenty – fifth in December. 圣诞节是十二月二十五日。

——Thanksgiving Day is the fourth Thursday in November. 感恩节是十一月第四个周四。

Explanatory Notes注释：

1. 英美人士表示日期有两种方式：

   1）英美人士用阿拉伯数字表示某年某月某日时，习惯有所不同。例如：2011 年 1 月 10 日。〔英国人〕1，10，2011 = 1st October，2011 =（the）first of October, two thousand eleven；〔美国人〕10，1，2011 = Jan（the）1st，2011 = January（the）first, two thousand eleven。为了避免这种误解，现在都采用罗马字表示月份，例如："10 月 1 日"写为 1/X，也可为 X/1，其意思均不会混淆。

   2）日期的写法有新旧之分，这点也得注意。例如：1994 年 2 月 25 日，旧式写为 25th Feb. 1994，这是由于旧的写法使用了序数词的缘故，所以凡有 st，nd，th 等序数词尾均为旧式写法；新式写法为 Feb 25. 1994。而当前最流行的形式则为先列月，次列日，再列年，例如：2，25，1994。

2. 英语表示年、月、日、星期、季节所用的介词很重要，有必要指出：

   1）在年前用介词 in。如：in nineteen seventy-three

   2）在月前用介词 in。如：in January/Jan.（月份第一个字母必须大写）

   3）在日前用介词 on。如：on the fifth

   4）在既有年又有月前仍然用介词 in。如：in Aug. nineteen-ninety-nine

   5）在有年、月、日的情况下，前面也要用介词 on。如：on Sept.（the）1st, nineteen ninety-eight.

   6）在星期前用介词 on。如：on Monday/Mon.（星期第一个字母必须大写）

   7）在季节前用介词 in。如：in spring.

   8）at 短语。如：at noon、at dust、at night、at daybreak、at midnight、at dawn.

3. 英语读几几年有一种习惯读法。这种读法是千位数的年份总和以二位二位地读。如：在 1999 年读作 in nineteen ninety-nine/in nineteen hundred and ninety-nine，但从不读 in one thousand nine hundred and ninety-nine。

Spoken Practice口语练习

1. Pair Work：

A acts as a Chinese builder. B acts as an inspector who wants to know when the project of International Trade Mansion will be started and what time it will be accomplished according to construction contract.

2. Answer the Following Questions in accordance with Practical Case：

1）Which year were you born，Tom？

2）What day（of the week）was（it）the day before yesterday？

3）What's the best season in your hometown？

4）What's the date today？

5）When is your birthday？

6）What's the date tomorrow？

3. Read & Interpret the Following Passage：

Special Greetings in USA

There're eight national holidays celebrated in the United States of America：New Year's Day（January），Washington's birthday（February），Memorial Day（May），the Fourth of July，Labor Day（September），Veteran's Day（November），Thanksgiving（November）and Christmas（December）. In addition，there're many state and local holidays.

4. Practise Reading the Following. Pay Attention to the Sense-groups and Pausing：

1）In 1960／the Chinese builders constructed a huge bridge／over the Changjiang River／at Nanjing.

2）All the students of our class／are practising／on the construction site／for the Building Engineering Group Corporation／which is one of the largest Corporation in China.

5. Fill in the Following Sentences with the Correct persations given and then put them into Chinese：

1）We usually have lunch ＿＿＿＿＿＿ twelve.

    A. in   B. at   C. on   D. for

2) Climate in Xi'an is very clear, it's cold _____ winter and hot
_____ summer.

    A. in   B. at   C. on   D. for

3) The highway & railway bridge must be completed _____ the end of
this year.

    A. in   B. on   C. before   D. after

4) My teacher of English was born _____ April 22, 1969.

    A. at   B. for   C. in   D. on

5) The People's Republic of China was founded _____ 1949.

    A. for   B. at   C. in   D. on

6) These students will be graduated _____ the age of 23.

    A. for   B in   C. at   D. on

7) The construction contract will become effective _____ 1/
X, 2008.

    A. in   B. to   C. at   D. on

8) I've physical culture class _____ Thursday and English classes
_____ Monday and Friday.

    A. to...to   B. on...on C. on...to D. above...to

9) The temperature today _____ Shanghai is twenty _____ zero.

    A. in...above B. for...in C. on...under D. at...over

10) My parants go to work _____ eight _____ the morning and
come back _____ six _____ the afternoon everyday.

    A. at...in, in...at   B. for...in, in...at

    C. at...in, at...in   D. at...in, for...in

6. Substitute the Following Words & Expressions:

1) Use the following **Day, Month, Season, Year** (日、月、季、年)
to replace the black words in the following sentence:

Jack: But what's the **date today**?

杰   克:今天几号啦?

Limi: **Today** is **December 30th, 2005.**

李   眯:今天是 **2005** 年 **12** 月 **30** 日。

Day, Month, Season, Year ［dei mʌnθ ˈsiːzn jiə］日、月、季节、年

date ［deit］日期

today ［təˈdei］今天

yesterday ［ˈjestədi］昨天

tomorrow ［təˈmɔrou］明天

the day before yesterday ［ðə dei biˈfɔːˈjestədi］前天

the day after tomorrow ［ðə dei ˈaːftə təˈmɔrou］后天

working day ［ˈwəːkiŋ dei］工作日

non-working day ［nʌn ˈwəːkiŋ dei］公休日

holiday ［ˈhɔlədei］节假日

solar calendar ［ˈsoulə ˈkælində］阳历

solar month ［ˈsoulə mʌnθ］太阳月

solar year ［ˈsoulə jiə］太阳年

lunar calendar ［ˈljuːnə ˈkælində］阴历

lunar month ［ˈljuːnə mʌnθ］太阴月（约29 1/2 日）

lunar year ［ˈljuːnə jiə］太阴年（约354 1/3 日）

the beginning of the year ［ðə biˈginiŋ əv ðə jiə］年初

the end of the year ［ðə end əv ðə jiə］年底

Anno Domini/A. D. ［ˈænou ˈdɔminai ei diː］公元后

before Christ /B. C. ［biˈfɔː kraist biː siː.］公元前

　 *　　　　　　*　　　　　　*

month ［mʌnθ］月份

January / Jan. ［ˈdʒænjuəri］一月/元月

February / Feb. ［ˈfebruəri］二月

March / Mar. ［maːtʃ］三月

April / Apr. ［ˈeiprəl］四月

May / May ［mei］五月

June / June ［dʒuːn］六月

July / Jul. ［dʒu(ː)ˈlai］七月

August / Aug. ［ˈɔːgəst］八月

September / Sept. ［səp'tembə］九月

October / Oct. ［ɔk'toubə］十月

November / Nov. ［nou'vembə］十一月

December / Dec. ［di'sembə］十二月

the beginning of the month ［ðə bi'giniŋ əv ðə mʌnθ］月初

the middle of the month ［ðə 'midl əv ðə mʌnθ］月中

the end of the month ［ðə end əv ðə mʌnθ］月底

this/ last/next month ［ðis laːst nekst mʌnθ］本/上/下月

*　　　　　　　*　　　　　　　*

season ［'siːzn］季节

winter ［'wintə］冬季

spring ［spriŋ］春季

summer ［'sʌmə］夏季

autumn/fall ［'ɔːtəm/fɔːl］秋季

2）Use the following **Day of the week**（星期）to replace the black words in the following sentences：

Jack：How time flies! In an instant, It's time for beginning the construction. And **what day is today**?

杰　克：时间过得可真快呀！转眼就到了开工时间。那**今天是星期几**？

Limi：Sorry. I'm too busy to care about it. Let me check the calendar. Oh, **today is Wednesday.**

李　睐：对不起，我还忙得没顾上这事，我得查一下日历。啊，**今天是星期三。**

day of the week ［dei əv ðə wiːk］**星期**

Monday/Mon. ［'mʌndi］星期一

Tuesday/Tue（s）. ［'tjuːzdi］星期二

Wednesday/Wed. ［'wenzdi］星期三

Thursday/Thu（rs）. ［'θəːzdi］星期四

Friday/Fri. ［'fraidi］星期五

Saturday/Sat. ［'sætədi］星期六

Sunday /Sun. ［ˈsʌndi］星期日

weekend ［ˈwiːkˈond］周末

weekday ［ˈwiːkdei］周日

this/next /last week ［ˈðis nekst laːst wiːk］本/下/上星期

Situational Dialogic Unit 20

第二十情景对话单元

Learn to Speak English

Talking about Time

Dave: Excuse me, what's the time by your watch, young man?

Amy: Oh, my watch has just been set by the radio time signal, it keeps good time.

Dave: Don't talk more. What time is it now, tell me quickly?

Amy: Listen, now it's two to two P. M.

Dave: I see. Oh, my watch is two minutes slow. Let me correct it. I've a meeting to attend and luckly meet you, or I'll be late for it. So I have to go at once. Bye!

Amy: OK. I'll say bye to you, too, because I'll return to my country by air at half past five P. M.

Dave: What did you say? Return to your country. Didn't I hear wrongly?

Amy: No, things happenned suddenly and I never leave without saying good-bye to you. It chances to see you while I'm going to telling you this.

Dave: That's all right. Will you come back then?

Amy: I'm sure to return. Half a month later, that's to say, at two to ten on 16th, Aug. I'll come back by the same flight.

Dave: Is that true, young man? I must meet you at the airport at that time.

Amy: Yes, it's true. Thank you first.

Dave: Not at all. In order not to miss plane, what's the time difference between Beijing time and the local time, I'd like to know?

Amy: Five hours, please remember it. I can come back as schedule time except special conditions.

学说英语

谈论时间

戴　维：对不起，年轻人。现在几点钟啦？

艾　米：啊，我的表是按电台的报时信号刚对的，分秒不差。

戴　维：再别贫嘴啦，快点告诉我现在到底是几点钟？

艾　米：听好了，现在是下午一点五十八分。

戴　维：我知道啦。啊，我的表慢了两分钟，让我对一对（表）吧。我有一个会议要参加，幸亏遇见您，要不然就迟到啦。我得赶紧走啊。再见！

艾　米：好吧，我也该给你告个别！因为今天下午五点半我乘飞机就要回国了。

戴　维：你说什么？回国，不会是我听错了吧？

艾　米：没听错，事情是有点突然，我绝不会不辞而别的。我正要向你告别，恰好就碰见你。

戴　维：没什么。那你还会来吗？

艾　米：我当然会来。半个月后，也就是8月16日晚九点五十八分我还是乘该航班返回。

戴　维：是吗，小伙子？到时我一定到机场接你。

艾　米：真的。先谢谢！

戴　维：没关系。为了不误接机时间，我想知道北京时间与当地时间的时差是多少？

艾　米：请记住时差是五个小时。我们会如期返回的，但特殊情况除外。

Dave: I believe this. And I worry if you go away and you're a statician and leave your statistical job. Who could come to do it then?

Amy: Thank you for your concerning. I go to my country to report our work. It'll take only fifteen days.

Dave: Fifteen days away, I know you must abserve your time and return as scheduled.

Amy: Sure. There's a budgeter who just came from my country two days ago, he can do statistical job, too. This won't affect normal work. Please set your mind at rest that every thing will be all right.

Dave: Budget and statistics couldn't be separated so he can hold two tasks at same time. That's OK. Naturally I can rest assured.

Amy: Good-bye, old chap.

Dave: Bye, my friend! Correct your watch, take your time. Hope you'll be plain sailing and have a good trip!

Amy: Thank you for your remind. Look forward to seeing you soon!

戴　维：我相信这点。你是统计员，我只是担心你走了，你的统计工作可咋办？谁来做这项工作？

艾　米：多谢你的关心。我是回国去汇报工作，仅离开 15 天。

戴　维：离开 15 天，我知道你一定会守时，如期归队的。

艾　米：这是肯定的。再说前两天从国内来了一位预算员，他也可以搞统计，不会影响正常工作的，请放心好啦，一切都会安排好的。

戴　维：预算和统计不分家，可以兼起来。这就好，我自然会放心的。

艾　米：再见吧，老兄！

戴　维：再见，我的好朋友！对准表，看好时间。祝您一帆风顺，旅途愉快！

艾　米：多谢你的提醒。盼望早点见到你！

Formulaic Communication 日常交际习语

Asking the Time and Responses 询问时间与应答

1. Does your watch keep good time? 你的表走得准吗？

——Yes, I think so. 是的，我想是。

2. Excuse me. What time is it now? /What's the time now? 对不起，现在几点钟了？

——It is/ It's seven thirty/half past seven. 现在是七点半。

3. At what time/When/What time is the meeting/class? 何时开会/上课？

——Time's up. It's time for meeting/class now. 时间到，该开会/上课了。

4. Could you tell me the time, sir? 先生，你能告诉我现在的时间吗？

——It's a quarter past six/ a quarter to six. 现在是六点一刻/五点四十五。

5. What's the time by your watch? 请问，你的表现在几点钟了？

——Sorry. I forget to wind up my watch. It's stopped. 对不起，我忘了上表，表停了。

——It's a little after eight. 我的表八点过一点。

Explanatory Notes 注释：

1. 英语中一般有两种表示时间的方法：

   1）**正读法**——先读小时，再读分钟，加上 A. M/a. m.（上午）用于区分 P. M/p. m.（下午）。这种读法与汉语表示时间法相同，这种表示法一般用于读课程表、列车时刻表等，即：**It's + 点钟 + 分钟**（+ A. M/a. m. or P. M/p. m.）。如：

   It's eight thirty A. M. 上午八点三十分。

   It's one fifty-eight P. M. 下午一点五十八分。

   2）**倒读法**——先读分钟再读点钟。这种读法与汉语表示时间法有所不同，应加以注意并养成习惯，即：**It's + 分钟 + to/past + 点钟**。如：

   It's half past/ eight. 八点半。It's two to / after two. 一点五十八分。如果分钟不超过半小时（1 – 30 分钟）用 past 或 before；如果分钟超过半小时（31 – 59 分钟）则用 to 或 after，如果是整点钟时还可在后加 o'clock；30 分钟用 half 表示，15 分钟用 a quarter 表示。

2. 北京（中国）时间与格林尼治时间相比差八小时，也就是说格林尼治时间是中午 12 时，北京时间应是 **12 + 8 = 20**，即下午 8 时。

3. It is two o'clock 现在是两点钟或 It is two 也可略 o'clock。还需要说明的是 o'clock 实际上是 of (the) clock 的省略形式，但在实际应用中往往省略。

4. Will you be here at eight o'clock tomorrom morning? 英语表示几时几刻的时间一定点用介词 **at**。如：at eight o'clock（在八点）。

5. **Listen，now it's two to two P. M.**

   P. M/p. m. = post meridiem 是拉丁语的缩写词，相当于英语的 afternoon 作下午解，表示的时间段应是从中午到午夜这段时间；而 A. M/a. m. = ante meridiem 也是拉丁语的缩写词，相当于英语的 before noon 作上午解，表示的时间段应是从午夜到中午这段时间。

6. 在一个单词前加了前缀，就改变了单词之意（即加前缀变词意）。

Spoken Practice 口语练习

1. Pair Work：

A is a site director（现场主任）. B is a resident engineer（驻地工程师）. A meets B on the way to construction site. A says we're about to have a production meeting. They talk somethings, for instance, B asks when the meeting will begin and what time it will finish.

2. Answer the Following Questions in accordance with Practical Case：

1）What time is it now?

2）When do you begin your first period of class every morning?

3）What time does your sister always go to work on the weekend?

4）When did you have your summer vocation last year?

5）When will you go to pay a visit to our construction site?

3. Read & Interpret the Following Passage：

Traditional Festivals and National Holidays in China

There're lunar and solar calendars in China. According to lunar calendar, there're mainly Spring Festival (1st of the first month of the Chinese lunar calendar), Lantern Festival (15th of the first month of the Chinese lunar calendar), Dragon-boat Festival (5th of the fifth month of the Chinese lunar calendar) and Mid-Autumn Festival / the Moon Festival (15th of the eighth month of the Chinese lunar calendar) and other tratditional festivals; In accordance with solar calendar, there're also New Year's Day (January 1st), International Women's Day (March / Mar. 8th), International Labour Day (May 1st), Youth Day (May 4th), Party Birth Day (Anniversary of the founding of the Communist Party of China) (July/Jul. 1st), Army Day (Anniversary of the founding of the Chinese People's Liberation Army) (August/Aug. 1st) and National Day (October/ Oct. 1st). Besides these, there're many local festivals and holidays in China.

4. Put the Following into Chinese or English with Two ways according to Expanatory Notes of This Unit：

1）咱们十点五分钟后见，老杨。

2）现在是一点五十八，离上班的时间还有两分钟。

3）现在是上午九点整，我们上第二节课的时间到了。

4）领导们，北京时间下午四点半开会。

5）我通常六点三十分起床、七点二十吃早饭、八点上课。

6）我父母总是早七点钟离家、七点五十到厂、八点正式工作。

5. **Given Prefixes（前缀）to Form Two Derivations（派生词）as Example：**

fore（预先，前）	forecast	foreknow	foresee
1）en（使）：	enlarge	_____	_____
2）re（重新）：	rebuild	_____	_____
3）super（超级，上层）：	superstructure		
4）sub（下面的）：	subway		
5）inter（之间的，互相的）：	international		
6）co（共同）：	co-operation		
7）post（在…之后的）：	post-graduate		
8）pre（预先，之前的）：	preface		
9）multi（多）：	multistorey		
10）auto（自）：	automobile		
11）tele（远距离）：	telephone		
12）trans（跨，移）：	transform		

6. **Substitute the Following Words & Expressions：**

Use the following **Terms about Time（时间相关用语）** to replace the black words in the following sentence：

Dave：Don't talk more. What **time** is it now, tell me quickly.

戴　维：再别贫嘴啦，快点告诉我现在到底是几**点钟**。

Amy: Listen, now it's **two to two** P. M.

艾　米：听好了，现在是下午**一点五十八分**。

Terms about Time ［tə:mz ə'baut 'taim］ 时间相关术语

o'clock ［ə'klɔk］ 钟点

hour ［'auə］ 小时

quarter ［'kwɔ:tə］ 刻钟

minute ['minit] 分钟

second ['sekənd] 秒钟

Beijing Time [beijing taim] 北京时间

Local Time ['loukl taim] 当地时间

Greenwish ['grinidʒ] 格林尼治（英国伦敦东南一市镇，本初子午线经过之地）

Greenwish Time ['grinidʒ taim] 格林尼治时

Greenwish Standard Time ['grinidʒ 'stændəd taim] 格林尼治标准时

Greenwish MeanTime/GMT ['grinidʒ miːn taim] 格林尼治平时

World Standard Time [wəːld 'stændəd taim] 世界标准时间

time difference [taim'difrəns] 时差

TEST Of PART TWO　第二部　测试题

1. Choose the Correct Answer and then Fill in the Blanks：

1）On a bus or train one must pay a _____.

    A. fee   B. charge   C. fare   D. dues

2）Which of the following words may be used as the opposite of **single** （room）_____.

    A. second   B. private   C. double   D. tired

3）Which is not **drinks** in the following _____？

    A. coffee   B. tea

    C. mineral water.   D. meat dumpling

4）The antonym for **get off** a train should be _____.

    A. get up   B. get on   C. take off   D. go down

5）Which of these is generally a synonym for **underground**, American English is _____.

    A. road   B. street   C. highway   D. subway

6）Which of the following words is correct spelling? _____.

    A. worksite   B. work site   C. working site   D. work-site

7）**To board a plane** means _____.

    A. to inspect a plane   B. to leave a plane

    C. to get on a plane   D. came into a plane

8）When a plane **takes off**, it _____, and when a plane **lands**, it _____.

    A. is down. . . is up   B. goes down. . . goes up

    C. lands. . . take off   D. goes up. . . goes down

9）Can you tell me the way to China Embassy, sir? Please go straight. The opposite of **go straight** here means _____.

    A. turn left   B. turn right

    C. turn aside   D. go ahead

10）A common synonym for **highroad**, Britain English means _____.

A. highway   B. underground

C. road   D. street

11) A common synonym for **hurry up** is _____.

 A. go slowly   B. step on it

 C. walk up   D. make haste

12) **By the rest of passengers** means _____ quickly board your plane, please.

 A. the remainder   B. those getting on

 C. some of persons   D. those getting off

13) When you check in a hotel, you'd better ask if the rate includes _____.

 A. breakfast and supper B. supper and dinner

 C. supper and lunch   D. breakfast and dinner

14) Which question is right answer of 'Today is December lst, 2001.'?

 A. What date is today? B. What time is it now?

 C. What's the date today? D. What's the date yesterday?

15) To **check in or check out** a hotel is to _____.

 A. pay one's bill and leave or arrive and register

 B. arrive and leave or pay one's bill and register

 C. check up or check with

 D. arrive and register or pay one's bill and leave

16) _____, can you help me, sir?

 A. Forgive me   B. Excuse me

 C. Pardon   D. Sorry

17) The builders in your worksite need to have a rest. Which sentence patten should be _____?

 A. SVP B. SVD   C. SVO.   D. SVoO

18) The following sentencese should be _____ 'Do be careful! Are you a manager or inspector? How time flies! We're students.'

 A. interrogative sentence/imperative sentence/exclamatory sentence/declarative sentence

B. exclamatory sentence/imperative sentence/declarative sentence/ interrogative sentence

C. interrogative sentence/imperative sentence/exclamatory sentenc/ declarative sentence

D. imperative sentence/interrogative sentence/exclamatory sentence/ declarative sentence

19) Need I aid you? Yes, you _____. May I photo here? No, you _____ . Must we help you? Yes, you _____. No, you _____.

A. need. needn't. must. needn't. B. must. mustn't. must. needn't.

C. must. needn't. must needn't. D. must. mayn't. must. needn't.

20) _____ beautiful buildings they are building! _____ the rain fell! _____ happy! _____ clean and tidy your construction site is!

A. What、How、How、How   B. What、How、What、How

C. How、What、How、What   D. How、How、What、What

2. Give the Following Words Chinese Meaning（Many Words in English Can Be Used as Nouns or Verbs. Here's a List of Such Words Learned in Part Two of Conversation）:

1) turn _____ n. _____ v.

2) plane _____ n. _____ v.

3) export _____ n. _____ v.

4) board _____ n. _____ v.

5) stop _____ n. _____ v.

6) taxi _____ n. _____ v.

7) train _____ n. _____ v.

8) watch _____ n. _____ v.

9) check _____ n. _____ v.

10) land _____ n. _____ v.

Write sentences with the words mentioned above as nouns and as verbs.

3. Complete the Following English Sentences with English Translation of Chinese Phrases Given：

1）Thak you for your . . . . 谢谢你的……。

①殷勤款待　　②忠告　　③邀请　　④关照　　⑤解释

2）Would you kindly . . . ? 您能……吗？

①停到这　　②进来　　③叫醒我　④给我们看看你们工地

3）Do you mind if I . . . ? 假如我……你不介意吗？

①打开门　②打开收音机　③开你的车　④打开电灯

4）Would you please. . . ? 你能……吗？

①和我一道去　②陪陪他　③再说一遍　④把你的名字写到这

5）Please remember me to. . . . 请替我向……问好。

①父母亲　　②老师　　③经理　　④老板

4. Make Sentences with the Following Phrases Given：

1）Let sb do. . . 　　_____

2）to be about to do. . . 　_____

3）to intend to do. . . 　_____

4）Would you mind doing. . . ? 　_____

5）both. . . and. . . 　_____

6）to be interested in. . . 　_____

7）look up. . . 　_____

8）Sorry to do. . . 　_____

9）to drop. . . into. . . 　_____

10）I'm afraid . . . 　_____

5. Fill in the Blanks with Proper Forms as Examples Given, and Learn All the Following Words by Heart：

	v.	n.	n.	adj.
1)	**construct**	**construction**	**constructor**	**constructive**
2)	contract	contraction	contractor	
3)	decorate	decoration		decorative
4)	translate	_____	translator	translative
5)	_____	action	actor	active

6）transform _____ transformer transformative

7）interpret interpretation _____ interpretive

8）produce production producer _____

6. Put the Following Words into Derivations（n. a. ad.）by Adding the Suffixes（后缀）Given：

（-ic，-some，-ward，-ful，-sive，-able，-al，-ance，-ent，-ly，-ics，-ably，-ence，-ant，-ize，-ity，-en，-sion）

Example：

press　　　　　　　pressure v.　　　　　　pressing　a.

1）electric _____ a. _____ n.

2）comprehen _____ a. _____ n.

3）assist _____ n. _____ a.

4）differ _____ a. _____ n.

5）comfort _____ ad. _____ a.

6）import _____ n. _____ a.

7）electron _____ a. _____ n.

8）internation _____ a.

9）modern _____ v.

10）up _____ ad.

11）deep _____ v.

12）fluent _____ ad.

13）trouble _____ a.

14）hope _____ a.

7. Fill in the Blanks and Then Learn the Following Compounds（Nouns）by Heart：

1）a. + n. = n. blueprint _____ _____

2）ad. + n. = n overcoat _____ _____

3）v. + n. = n break-water _____ _____

4）n. + ving. = n. handwriting _____ _____

5）v. + ad. = n. break-down _____ _____

6）n. + prep. phr. = n. editor-in-chief _____

7）v. ing + n. = n.　waiting-room 　＿＿＿＿＿＿　＿＿＿＿＿＿

8）n. + n. = n.　worksite 　＿＿＿＿＿＿　＿＿＿＿＿＿

8. *Supposing You're a Builder and Work abroad. Try to say Something about Your Eating, Staying, Shopping, Working, sight-seeing, Going by Air/Bus/Train and So on in English as more as possible.*

Appendix Ⅰ　附录Ⅰ

The International Phonetic Symbols
国际音标

Vowels ['vauəlz]　　　　　元音（共20个）

1. front vowels [frʌnt 'vauəlz]

  [i:]　street [stri:t] 街道

  [i]　building ['bildiŋ] 建筑物

  [e]　bedroom ['bedru:m] 卧室

  [æ]　balcony ['bælkəni] 阳台

2. central vowels ['sentrəl 'vauəlz]

  [ə]　mansion ['mænʃən] 大厦，宅第

  [ə:]　church [tʃə:tʃ] 教堂

3. back vowels [bæk 'vauəlz]

  [a:]　garden ['ga:dn] 花园

  [ʌ]　study ['stʌdi] 书房

  [ɔ]　office ['ɔfis] 办公室

  [ɔ:]　hall [hɔ:l] 大厅

  [u]　footing ['futiŋ] 基脚

  [u:]　room [ru:m] 房间

4. falling diphthongs ['fɔ:liŋ 'difθɔŋz]

  [ei]　basement ['beismənt] 地下室

  [ai]　dining hall ['dainiŋ hɔ:l] 餐厅

  [ɔi]　toilet ['tɔilit] 厕所

  [au]　house [haus] 房屋

  [əu]　road [rəud] 道路

5. rising diphthongs ['raiziŋ 'difθɔŋz]

  [iə]　theatre ['θiətə] 剧院

  [ɛə]　staircase ['stɛəkeis] 楼梯间

  [uə]　tower ['tauə] 塔

---

1. 前元音（4个）

  eaves [i:vz] 屋檐

  ridge [ridʒ] 屋脊

  exit ['eksit] 出口

  bræcket ['brækit] 牛腿

2. 中元音（2个）

  canopy ['kænəpi] 雨篷

  girder ['gə:də] 大梁

3. 后元音（6个）

  arch [a:tʃ] 拱

  truss ['trʌs] 屋架

  column ['kɔləm] 柱

  floor [flɔ:] 地板/面

  hook [huk] 吊钩

  roof [ru:f] 屋顶

4. 合口双元音（5个）

  gable ['geibl] 山墙

  spire ['spaiə] 尖塔

  alloy ['ælɔi] 合金

  foundation [faun'deiʃən] 基础

  window ['windəu] 窗

5. 集中双元音（3个）

  pier [piə] 墙墩子

  air [ɛə] 柱子

  bower ['bauə] 凉亭

Consonant ［ˈkɔnsənənt］　　　　　辅音（共 28 个）

1, plosive consonants ［ˈpləusiv ˈkɔnsənənts］

［p］	pipe ［paip］ 管子	plane ［plein］ 刨子
［b］	bulb ［bʌlb］ 灯泡	barrow ［ˈbærəu］ 手推车
［t］	tile ［tail］ 瓦	tool ［tuːl］ 工具
［d］	wood ［wud］ 木料	die ［dai］ 板牙
［k］	concrete ［ˈkɔnkriːt］ 混凝土	axe ［æks］ 斧子
［g］	glass ［glaːs］ 玻璃	gauge ［geidʒ］ 量器

1. 爆破音（6 个）

2. nasal consonants ［ˈneizəl ˈkɔnsənənts］

［m］	mortar ［ˈmɔːtə］ 灰浆	mixer ［ˈmiksə］ 搅拌机
［n］	nut ［nʌt］ 螺母	punch ［pʌntʃ］ 冲子
［ŋ］	bearing ［ˈbɛəriŋ］ 轴承	centering ［ˈsentəriŋ］ 拱架

2. 鼻音（3 个）

3. fricative consonants ［ˈfrikətiv ˈkɔnsənənts］

［f］	fuse ［fjuːz］ 保险丝	knife ［naif］ 刀子
［v］	valve ［vælv］ 阀门	level ［ˈlevl］ 水准仪
［θ］	thinner ［ˈθinə］ 稀释剂	theodolite ［θiˈɔdəlait］ 经纬仪
［ð］	lathe ［leið］ 车床	father ［ˈfaːðə］ 创始人
［s］	cement ［siˈment］ 水泥	saw ［sɔː］ 锯子
［z］	mosaic ［mouˈzeiik］ 马赛克	chisel ［ˈtʃizl］ 錾凿
［ʃ］	warnish ［ˈvaːniʃ］ 清漆	brush ［brʌʃ］ 刷子
［ʒ］	measure ［ˈmeʒə］ 量具	garage ［ˈgæraːʒ］ 汽车库
［r］	rivet ［ˈrivit］ 铆钉	ruler ［ˈruːlə］ 直尺
［h］	handle ［ˈhændl］ 拉手	hammer ［ˈhæmə］ 锤子

3. 摩擦音（10 个）

4. affricate consonants ［ˈæfrikit ˈkɔnsənənts］

［tʃ］	switch ［switʃ］ 开关	wrench ［wentʃ］ 扳手
［dʒ］	flange ［flændʒ］ 法兰	jack ［dʒæk］ 千斤顶
［ts］	bolts ［bouts］ 插销	floats ［flouts］ 抹子
［dz］	goods ［gudz］ 货物	hobs ［hɔbz］ 灰斗
［tr］	petrol ［ˈpetrəl］ 汽油	trowel ［ˈtrauəl］ 泥瓦刀
［dr］	drain ［drain］ 排水管	drill ［drill］ 钻子

4. 破擦音（6 个）

5. semi-vowels ［ˈsemi ˈvauəlz］

［w］	wire ［ˈwaiə］ 铁丝	welder ［ˈweldə］ 焊机
［j］	union ［ˈjuːnjən］ 活接头	unit ［ˈjuːnit］ 元/部件

5. 半元音（2 个）

6. lateral consonants ［ˈlætərəl ˈkɔnsənəntz］

［l］	nail ［neil］ 钉子	ladder ［ˈlædə］ 梯子

6. 旁流音（1 个）

Explanatory Notes 注释：

1. 英语国际音标是由国际语言学协会规定的一套音标（本书的注音均采用国际音标）。由此可见国际音标在英语这一语种的地位，也不难看出它在英语学习，特别是口语中的统一性、规范性、基础性以及重要性。英语国际音标在某种程度上和汉语拼音方案一样。判断一个人的汉语讲得是否标准的依据应是对其汉语拼音发音来决定；同样判断一个人的英语讲得是否标准的依据也应是对其英语国际音标发音来决定。鉴别一个人，特别是初学者是否有汉语自学基础，也要看其对汉语拼音方案是否掌握。如果掌握了，在无人帮助的情况下，打开注有拼音的书籍也能准确无误地读出每个字的音，这一道理对于英语学习也是不言而喻的；所以学好英语国际音标不仅有上述好处，而且还能更快、更有效、更准确地进行英语单词的拼写。因此学好国际音标是学好英语最起码的要求，其重要性就好比在没有坚实的基础上建起的高楼大厦，楼房的质量就可想而知。

2. 英语的拼音方法有两种，学好国际音标加之掌握了这两种方法才能拼读好英语单词。

1）辅音在前，元音在后时，两音要相拼。**先做好发该辅音的口形，然后从这一口形发出元音，中间不能停顿。**

如 [p] - [i:] — [pi:]，[d] - [ai] — [dai]。

2）元音在前，辅音在后时，**连续发出各自的音。**

如 [e] — [g] — [eg]，[a:] — [m] — [a：m]。

Appendix Ⅱ 附录Ⅱ

Comparison between British & American Useful Words
英美英语常用词语对照

美国英语惯用词 American Usage	英语对应词 English Equivalent	汉语词意 Chinese Meaning
alumnus	graduate	毕业生
apartment	flat	一套房间，公寓
apartment house	block of flats	公寓楼
automobile	motorcar, car	汽车
baggage	luggage	行李
bar	pub	酒吧
belt road	ring road	环行公路
bid	tender	投标
bidder	tenderer	投标人
bill	note	钞票
billion	milliard	十亿
biscuit	scone, bread – roll	饼干
bond	stock	债券
buzz saw	circular saw machine	圆锯
cab/taxicab	taxi	出租车
call you	phone/ring you	打电话给你
can (of fruit, etc.)	tin	罐头
candy	sweets	糖果
car (on railway)	carriage	车辆
checking account	current account	活期存款
closet	cupboard	碗碟橱
conductor (of a train)	guard	列车员
corn	maize	五谷
cracker	cheese biscui	乳酪饼干
daylight – saving time	summer time	夏令时间

续表

美国英语惯用词 American Usage	英语对应词 English Equivalent	汉语词意 Chinese Meaning
adeck of cards	a pack of cards	一副纸牌
deposit account	savings account	定期存款
derby	bowler hat	圆顶礼帽
drug－store	chemist's shop	药店
dump car	trough tipper	翻斗车
elevator	lift	电梯，卷扬机
engineer（of a train）	engine driver	（火车）司机
expressway	motorway	高速公路
fall	autumn	秋季
faucet	water－tap	水龙头
first floor	ground floor	楼下/第一层楼
football game	football match	足球赛
freight car	goods wagon	货车
freight elevator	goods lift	运货电梯
gas，gasoline	petrol	汽油
gear－shift	sear－lever	变速装置
generator	dyname	发电机
grip	traveling bag	旅行袋
highway	mainroad	公路
hostess	waitress	女招待，服务员
kerosene	paraffin	煤油
last/family/second name	surname	姓氏
long－distance call	trunk call	长途电话
lumber	sawn timber	板材
mail	post（letters）	邮件
mailbox	postbox	邮箱
mailman/carrier	postman	邮递员
math	maths	数学
motor	engine	发动机
movies	pictures/film	电影

续表

美国英语惯用词 American Usage	英语对应词 English Equivalent	汉语词意 Chinese Meaning
muffler	scarf	围巾
one way	single（ticket）	单程票
overpass	flyover	立体交叉
package	postal parcel	邮政包裹
pants	trousers	裤子
period	full stop	句号
porch，piazza	veranda(h)	骑楼
potato chips	crips	（油炸马铃）薯条
public house	inn	小旅馆
purse	lady's hand - bag	（女士）手提包
railroad	railway	铁路
reserve	book	预定
roundtrip ticket	return ticket	往返票
rug	parpet	地毯
second floor	first floor	二楼/第二层楼
Secretary of State	Foreign Secretary	外交大臣
schedule	timetable	时间/刻表
sedan	saloon car	小轿车
sick	ill	有病的
sidewalk	pavement，foot - path	人行道
solid color	plain colour	单色
State Department	Foreign Office	外交部
stock	share	股票
stoker	fireman	司炉
stove	cooker	炉
streetcar	tram	有轨电车
subway	underground	地铁
subway station	underground station	地铁车站
sun visor	sun shield	遮日板
superhighway	motor way	高速公路

续表

美国英语惯用词 American Usage	英国对应词 English Equivalent	汉语词意 Chinese Meaning
telephone book	telephone directory	电话号码簿
the Administration	the Government	政府
traffic circle	roundabout	环行交叉
truck	lorry/van	卡车
turn – out lane	waiting bay	停车候车道
windshield	windscreen wiper	风挡刮水器
wreck	accident	事故
weather predication	weather forecast	天气预报
Y – intersection	Y – junction	Y 字形交叉

Explanatory Notes 注释：

英美用词不同是英美英语不同之一，也是一个不争的事实，可这一点往往使人不可思议，所以也就未必能接受。为了确保今后口语会话，特别是听力水平的提高，这里列出了部分英美不同的用词，其目的就是让读者知道，一个汉语意思却有两个不同的英语单词，即英国英语用词和美国英语用词。

Appendix Ⅲ 附录Ⅲ

Points for Attention when Chinese Associates with Westener
中国人与西方人士交往应注意的事项

1. 西方/英美人士认为周五（Friday）这天是一周最不吉利的一天，所以最忌讳把社交活动安排在这一天。

2. 西方/英美人士初次交往，最忌讳询问对方的芳名（What's your name?）。

3. 西方/英美人士初次见面，寒暄时，最忌讳使用：您的职业是什么？（What do you do for a living?），你去哪儿？（Where are you going?），你吃饭了吗？（Have you eaten yet?）这些问语。

4. 西方/英美人士忌讳别人随便问你多大了？（How old are you?）

5. 西方/英美人士忌讳别人了解他/她的婚姻状况，问您结婚了吗？（Are you married?）

6. 西方/英美人士忌讳别人打听他/她的收入，问您的收入是多少？（How much do you earn?）

7. 西方/英美人士忌讳别人打听他/她的地址，问您住在哪儿？（Where do you live?）

8. 西方/英美人士忌讳未经主人许可，就进入住宅。

9. 西方/英美人士忌讳男人抢先。在男女一起出没在公共场合时，如上车、进门、就座等场合，不论年龄大小。应让女士先行和女士优先（Ladies, first!）。

10. 西方/英美人士忌讳约会不按时到或不到的失约。

11. 西方/英美人士忌讳突然拜访。

12. 西方/英美人士忌讳身着睡衣去迎接客人。

13. 西方/英美人士忌讳称呼黑人（Negro），而应称之为（Black）。

14. 西方/英国人士忌讳用人像作商标或装潢。

15. 西方/英美人士忌讳打扰了某人、碰坏了某物、踩了某人脚等错事一走了之，而应说句"对不起"（Sorry）。

16. 西方/英美人士忌讳见面时说"吃了吗?"（Have you eaten yet?）而应根据不同的时间和场合说"Good moorning /afternoon/evening! ..."；忌讳在分别是说"我走了。"（I must go.）应说"再见"（Good – bye!）

17. 西方/英美人士忌讳说"I and you⋯.""I, my mother and my father⋯."而说"You and me⋯." "My mother、my father and I⋯." 等把"I"排列在倒数第一位。这和中国人的习惯说法"我和你⋯。""我和我父母⋯。"正好相反，中国人则把"我"排列在正数第一位。

18. 西方/英美人士忌讳把"I"写成"i"，这也许是自信的表示。

19. 西方/英美人士忌讳先将妇女介绍给男士，将年长者介绍给年轻人，将身份高贵的人介绍给身份低下的人。切记正确的介绍顺序应该是将男士先介绍给女士，将年轻人先介绍给年长者，将儿童介绍给成人，将未婚者介绍给已婚者，将身份低下的人先介绍给身份高贵的人即将一般人介绍给重要人，然后再把后者介绍给前者。而对于身份高贵者，不要轻易把别人介绍他/她，而应先征得他/她的同意。

20. 西方/英美人士忌讳初次见面谈话就打听个人私事，而常以谈论天气为最佳话题（A very common way to start a conversation is to talk about the weather in the Western countries, especially in Britain.）。

21. 西方/英美人士忌讳过分的客气或虚情假意。由于英美人士一般都很直率，所以到别人家做客，主人端来吃的或喝的东西，想吃或想喝，就说"Yes. Thank you.",反之就说"No. Thank you."。如果你说了"No. Thank you.",他们绝不会像中国人那样再三让你了。

22. 西方/英美人士忌讳别人为你服务后、向你赠送礼物后、或归还了钱物时说"没什么"，但必须说"谢谢你""Thank you"。

23. 西方/英美人士忌讳在离开晚会时，过分客气要握手。切记这种告别通常不必握手。

24. 西方/英美人士忌讳询问情况或打扰别人时搭话，而有礼貌的方式应该说声"请原谅。"（Excuse me.）

25. 西方/英美人士忌讳 13 人同桌就餐。

26. 英美人士忌讳用餐时，打嗝、松裤带。

27. 西方/英美人士忌讳在餐桌上用牙签，通常餐后用。

28. 西方/英美人士忌讳在西餐桌上用餐时，把食物放进口中再吐出来，也就是一口吃不下的一块肉等类食物先咬一部分剩下的放在盘中待吃下口中的再吃剩在盘中的，而应先在盘中用刀切成小块，把一块一块的吃视为文明之举。

29. 西方/英美人士忌讳在西餐桌上用餐时，该动手时却不用手而用刀叉。如拿面包应用手拿而不用叉子去叉，吃整只龙虾应用手剥壳而用刀叉剥壳，这种用刀叉也是一种失礼。

30. 西方/英美人士忌讳在席间或用餐时见了好吃的或主人亲手做的饭菜就闷着头不吱声的吃呀喝呀，而应在用餐期间或饭后赞赏酒菜点心以表示对主人所做的一切的肯定和理解。

【注】如果西方/英美人士的风俗习惯使中国人觉得奇怪，别忘了中国人到世界其他国家生活，也会有同样的感觉。在世界上不同民族都生活在不同文化之中，所以日常的行为有许多互不相同的。是的，假如不是这样，这个世界将是多么单调无味啊！而有些差别是正常的，也是客观存在，但必须正视现实虚心去学，从不习惯到习惯。这就是列举中国人与西方人士交往应注意的事项的初衷，供读者学习和借鉴，以免和西方人士交往时少出或不出笑话，做到入乡随俗，搞好外事工作。

Appendix IV 附录 IV

Key to Spoken Practice　口语练习答案
Chinese Reference Translation　汉语参考译文

第一部　建筑校园英语情景会话

第一情景对话单元

卡尔·马克思是怎样学外语的

"外语是人生斗争的武器"是卡尔·马克思的名言。他是这样说的也是这样做的。马克思能阅读欧洲所有主要的语言并能用德语、法语和英语三种语言进行写作。

马克思50岁时才开始学俄语，而且六个月后他就能阅读著名的作家果戈理和普希金的著作。

第二情景对话单元

我们的学院

我们的学院位于市郊，离城并不十分遥远，交通方便，环境幽雅。学院有二十几栋教学大楼和公寓楼、两个图书馆、许多实验室、一栋办公大楼、礼堂、科学馆、体育馆和一个大运动场。院方为学子们营造一个学习、生活的良好氛围。

第三情景对话单元

美国英语和英国英语的区别

可能许多人并不知道美国英语和英国英语还有下列三大区别：

1. 拼写区别。例如，英国英语使用的单词 colour、centre and travelled 等词的拼写，在美国英语中则拼写为 color、center and traveled。

2. 发音区别。比如，美国人发 dance 为［dæns］、not 为［nat］、hurry 为［ˈhə.ri］然而英国人却发 dance 为［daːns］、not 为［nɔt］、hurry 为［ˈhʌːri］。

3. 用词（语）区别。例如，美国人用 gas、mail、right away、I guess 等，但英国人却用 petrol、post、at once、I think。

第四情景对话单元

怎样学好英语

为了学好一种语言，一个人不仅要掌握词汇和发音，以及一系列造句的规则，还应对语法做到差不多基本融会贯通。但是仅仅学习语法还不能说就是掌握一种语言。如果只学到语法这一点，那你学到的可能只是语法，而不是语言。相反记住大量句子并学会如何使用这些句子，就能既学会语法，又学会语言。

第五情景对话单元

国际通用语言——英语

英语是国际通用语言之一。根据 1986 年的统计数据，世界上把英语作为母语的人已超过四亿。包括英国、美国、加拿大、新西兰以及澳大利亚，世界上还有二十多个国家把英语作为官方语言和第二语言，世界上近五分之一的人在某种程度上都讲英语。

从英语使用的范围来看，世界上 70% 以上的邮政、广播节目，大部分科技资料，绝大多数国际会议都以英语为第一通用语言。英语自然是联合国正式的工作语言之一。

第六情景对话单元

求职书

中国 上海 第 1696 号信箱
2008 年 5 月 18 日

美国纽约 N.Y. 1000197
理查德建筑公司 第 6959 号信箱

先生：

阅读了今天日报广告栏目，得知贵公司招聘建筑工程技术人员，特冒昧自荐。本人简历如下：

出生地：中国上海

年龄：22 岁

要求工资：1000 美元/月

文化程度：建筑工程学院毕业

求职的原因：我学习的专业是工业与民用建筑，为谋求学以致用，我觉得这一职务有利于本人的提高和发展。

如上述条件尚能符合贵公司的要求，请约期面谈。

盼望能早日回音，不胜感谢。

你们恭顺的

刘华

第七情景对话单元

建筑生产工种

建筑生产中有四大工种，这四大工种是土（木）建（筑）工人、建筑安装工人、建筑机械工人和建筑装饰工人。当然，每一大工种都包括八种以上的工种。例如：建筑安装工人可分为水暖工、电工、焊工、起重工、通风工、铆工、安装钳工等工种。各工种之间密切配合，缺一不可。每一工种都在建筑施工中起着重要的作用。

第八情景对话单元

办公自动化

当今的机关团体配置了各种各样的办公自动化的硬、软件。这些配置都试图使目前手工完成的任务和功能自动化。但专家认为要达到办公自动化的关键在于集成——将各种硬、软件紧密结合成一个完整的系统，使得计算机、通信设备和办公设备联网。办公人员就能方便的通过自己桌面上的计算机访问整个系统时，办公自动化这个目标就可实现。

第九情景对话单元

AutoCAD 的基础知识

因为 AutoCAD 可以实现个性化以满足不同用户的需求，所以很受宠爱。在 AutoCAD 的屏幕上显示有：

1. 标题栏——这将向你展示正在运行的程序名以及当前文件名。2. 下拉菜单——这些是标准的下拉菜单，通过它们可以访问全部的命令。3. 主要的工具栏——这既有指挥常用的 AutoCAD 命令又有大部分的标准 Windows 按钮。4. 制图空间——这是你拥有一个几乎是无限大制图的地方。5. 状态栏——这里可允许查看或改变图面的不同模式。

TEST OF PART ONE　第一部　测试题

5. A：Where are you going?

　 B：I'm going **to Worksite.**

　 A：**What** are you going **for**?

　 B：I'm going **for Woking.**

　 A：Are you **in a hurry**?

　 B：I'm rather in a hurry.

第二部　建筑施工人员国外生活英语情景会话

第十情景对话单元

复合词是怎样形成的

一个长着一双蓝眼睛的女孩就是蓝眼睛女孩。长得好看的孩子就是好看孩子。你称一位穿着很讲究的人什么人？（穿着）讲究人。如果为了不使声音穿过房间的地板、墙壁和顶棚，我们应该说这是隔声室。这就是英语复合词怎样形成的方法。在将来的学习过程中尽量采用这种方法学习英语词语，会很快扩大你的词汇量，从而达到事半功倍的学习效果。

第十一情景对话单元

怎样使用 Mr. Mrs. Miss. Ms. 甚至 Sir, Madam

几乎每个人都认识 Mr. = Mister，Mrs. = Mistress，Miss，Ms 甚至也认识 Sir，Madam，但也许有些人并不十分懂得怎样使用这些词，也不清楚怎样发其音。

Mrs = Mistress 应放在已婚女性姓氏之前，发［'misiz］音。男性姓氏之前，我们应选用 Mr. = Mister 发［'mistə］音。对于未婚女子姓氏前应使用 Miss，发［mis］音。可是 Mr. = Mister 这个单词并没有表露出一位男性是否结婚，因此许多女性认为这对于人类来说是一种进步，所以女性也要以同样的方式和男性平等相待。妇女们认为人们也没有必要知道女性是否结婚。然而，当今许多妇女并不喜欢用 Mrs. 或 Miss，更喜欢用 Ms.［miz］这个称呼词。

这些是上述提到的这四个词的用法。而 Sir 用于称呼男性为先生，无需加姓或名；Madam 则是对女性'夫人''太太'的称呼，也不需要加姓或名，但人们常说 Dear Sir/Madam 却是对的。

第十二情景对话单元

问　路

假如你要问路的话，人们通常是会乐意相告的。但你应尽量掌握准确地址，而且越具体越好。尽管所有的住户房屋都有门牌，但对于许多房屋的住户，人们却只知其名而不知其址。假如你找这样的住户有困难的话，电话号码簿却是最常用作查找地址的资料。须知，许多城市和一些城镇通常都是按街区建造而成的，人们常会这样告诉陌生人，比如说："过一两个街区，然后再向左拐。"

第十三情景对话单元

什么是（里程收费）表？

（里程收费）表是出租车中的一种装置。每当出租车载客出发时，一面小旗就树立起来，表就开始工作了。里程表记录着车所行走的里程，同时显示出准确的费收数额，乘客就会根据数额付给车费。当今出租车都已安装有这种装置，这样对于顾客而言就能明白消费合理消费。

第十四情景对话单元

地 铁

当今世界上许多大城市都有地铁，以便乘客出行方便起见，城市地铁都有一个四通八达而且相当复杂的地铁快速转运网。每列地铁都用字母或数字表示供乘客识别。地铁的票价也不固定，而是按行程远近来确定的。所以乘客必须持票才能上站台，有时备有如数的零钱也行。

第十五情景对话单元

忠 告

各家旅馆（或饭店），无论是一般旅馆，星级饭店、还是汽车旅馆，收费标准完全不同。在预订或居住之前，最好了解清其价格，再作出决定，这才是一个明智之举。

第十六情景对话单元

中国饭馆

亚洲人，特别是中国人到了西方国家会惊奇的看到也有大量的中国饭馆在此，每个城市或乡镇至少都有一家。这些饭馆供应价廉物美的饭菜和小吃而颇受欢迎。但你得自己订购所需的食品，自己端到餐桌上。假如你订购'带走'食品，你也可以拿出店外。

在这种店无需付小费，这点也得在此告诉你。

第十七情景对话单元

世界旅游胜地——西安

西安，历史上称之为长安，是中华文化的源头，中华文化的代表，浓缩了五千年中华文明的遗传基因。唐长安城是中国第一个国际化大都市，西安的国际化特色就是具有中国气质的文化。由于西安历经了周、汉、隋、唐等十三个朝代，跨越1100多年的漫长历史，是中国建都朝代最多，建都时间最长的最古老的都城，同样是世界上四大古都之一。自汉朝起，西安就已是中国同世界许多国家之间进行交往的重要城市，也是丝绸之路的起点，它促进了汉以及汉以后国际化经济和文化的交流。西安以其文化遗产和艺术宝库著称于世，所以西安是座世界城市，文化之都，因此也早已成为世界最著名的旅游胜地之一。常言道：到中国旅游，没到过西安就等于没到过中国。所以每年都有数以千万计的游客来西安旅游观光。

第十八情景对话单元

天 气

从谈论天气开始，这在西方许多国家是一种极其普通的交谈方式，特别是在英国，这一点同中国人相比是完全不同的交谈方式。其原因不只是因为气候有趣和多变，而且是因为英国人不愿意同不是亲友的人谈论私事。不管在任何地方与一个陌生人谈论天气都是一种既有用又不会伤害别人的交谈方式。为了更好的交往，我们中国人应懂得这一点。

第十九情景对话单元

美国特定时节的问候

美国有八个全国性庆祝节日。这些节日是：元旦（一月），华盛顿诞辰纪念日（二月），阵亡将士纪念日（五月），美国独立纪念日（七月四日），劳动节（九月），退伍军人节（十一月），感恩节（十一月），以及圣诞节（十二月）。除此之外，还有各州自定的和地区性的许多节日。

第二十情景对话单元

中国的传统节日和公共节假日

在中国，有农历和阳历之分。依照农历主要有（农历正月初一）春节，（农历正月十五）元宵节/灯笼节，（农历五月初五）五月端午节，（农历八月十五）中秋节等传统节日；然而根据阳历通常却有元旦（一月一日），国际妇女节（三月八日），青年节（五月四日），国际劳动节（五月一日），党的生日（中国共产党成立纪念日）（七月一日），建军节（中国人民解放军建军纪念日）（八月一日），国庆节（十月一日），除了上述节假日外，在中国还有很多地方节假日。

TEST OF PART TWO　第二部　测试题

1. 1）hospitality　　2）advance　　　3）invitation
　 4）attention　　　5）explaining
2. 1）stop here　　　2）come in
　 3）wake me up　　4）show us to your site
3. 1）open the door　2）turn on your radio
　 3）drive your car　4）switch on the electric lamp.
4. 1）go with me　　2）accompany him
　 3）say it again　　4）write down your name here
5. 1）parents　　　　2）teacher
　 3）manager　　　4）boss